Praise for

HARD QUESTIONS, HEART ANSWERS

HARD

QUESTIONS,

HEART

ANSWERS

SPEECHES AND SERMONS

THE REVEREND
BERNICE A. KING

BROADWAY BOOKS, NEW YORK

BROADWAY

First trade paperback edition published 1997.

Designed by Fearn Cutler

License for quotes of Dr. Martin Luther King Jr. is granted by Intellectual Properties Management, Atlanta, Georgia, as the manager for the King estate.

The Library of Congress has catalogued the hardcover edition as:

King, Bernice A.

Hard questions, heart answers / Bernice A. King. — 1st ed.

p.   cm.

ISBN 0-553-06710-9 (hardcover)

1. Baptists—Sermons.   2. Sermons, American—Afro-American authors.
3. Sermons, American—Women authors.   4. United States—Moral conditions.   5. United States—Race relations.   I. Title.

BX6333.K546F67   1996

251′.06—dc20   96–19690

CIP

ISBN 0-7679-0037-5

99 00 01 10 9 8 7 6 5 4 3 2

This book is dedicated to my late father, Martin Luther King Jr.,
whose spoken and written words have inspired many of my thoughts.

CONTENTS

ACKNOWLEDGMENTS

This book is an answered prayer. In the fall of 1993, after a conversation with my publicist concerning ways to get my message out to people beyond my listening audience, I started praying. I did not realize that an interview with the *New York Times,* in January 1994, would be the door to introduce me to not only my literary agent, Kim Witherspoon, but other agents as well. Initially, I thought that this was too good to be true, but then I caught myself. I remember that God's ways are not our ways and his thoughts are not our thoughts. Ordinarily a person in my position would be knocking on the doors of opportunity, but in this case, the door of opportunity was opened to me before I could knock. Therefore I first and foremost want to thank God from whom all of my blessings flow. He's a definite matchmaker.

My heartfelt gratitude belongs to my mother, whose unconditional and never-ending love and support propels me to undertake projects like this book—I know she's got my back.

I am especially appreciative of my siblings, Yolanda, Martin, and Dexter, for believing in their little sister and encouraging me over the years to speak what's on my mind. You're right, Dexter, it's hard for me to be silent, now that my heart's convicted.

Finally I want to extend my thanks to the following for their individual contributions to this book: Bonita Ingram, Melanie Bacon, Debbie Black, all of whom spent countless hours typing the manuscript; Karen Ross, Beverly James— my staff who worked with me on some of the finishing touches; Timothy McDonald and Steve Klein for your research and writing assistance; Hilda Tompkins for your ideas; my Pastor, Byron L. Broussard, for your prayers, patience, and understanding while I worked on this book; my church family, Greater Rising Star Baptist Church, for your prayers; Kim Witherspoon, my literary agent, for your input; my editor, John Sterling, for understanding my heart and seeking to offer suggestions in line with it; Anthony S. Frierson for encouraging me to do the *New York Times* article and for working on my behalf with Kim and John; and my listening audience for your support, prayers, and encouragement to make my speeches and sermons available. To God Be the Glory.

INTRODUCTION

Do you remember the cliché, "Sticks and stones may break my bones, but words will never hurt me"? I remember hearing these words uttered from my mother's mouth after being insulted by a playmate. For a long time, I believed that words would never hurt me. This belief kept me out of a lot of fights and heated exchanges as a child; I'm sure it sometimes spared the shedding of blood. But, I have shed many tears because of some of the words I heard as a child. Fortunately, with the passage of time and help of word therapy, the emotional pain and suffering that I experienced as a result of these hurtful words has diminished.

I now realize that words are not only powerful, but critical to life. They can lift you up or let you down. They can save you from a tragic outcome or lead you to a triumphant result. In some instances, words have made the difference between life and death. In fact, the Holy Bible informs us that life and death are in the power of the tongue.

In other words, what comes out of our mouths can speak life or death into situations and circumstances.

My father, Martin Luther King Jr., is remembered as a man who had a way with words. His words caused America to change its thinking about and behavior toward people of color and lesser means. His words galvanized many into a movement for change. People were inspired to rise from their seats of complacency and their beds of oppression because of my daddy's words. He was indeed a master of the King's English, but his oratory was more than merely inspiring. He touched the lives of people because his words penetrated their very hearts.

People often make comparisons between my way of speaking and my father's. They say that I sound like him; that I remind them of him; that many of my words resonate with the same passion as his. While I don't mind these comparisons, I'm not always sure I know what people mean by them. After all, I barely knew my father.

I was only five when Daddy was assassinated. As a child, I was shy and withdrawn. I seldom asked questions about my father. Not until my early twenties did I begin to read his books and listen to his speeches and sermons, famous and not so famous. Suddenly his powerful words mattered to me very much. I was in theology school then and had already been giving speeches for about five years.

It is now almost seventeen years since I first started giving speeches. I have spoken to thousands of people—African American, White American, Asian American, Hispanic American, and Native American. While the words I have spoken have not hurt people—at least, I don't think they have—

I know they have pierced some hearts and caused some to say "ouch." The response I often receive from listeners is "You touched my heart." I believe this is the real connection between me and my father—our words flow from a heart full of love, compassion, and conviction, out to the hearts of others. Like my father, I desire to be an instrument to convert the hearts of men, women, boys, and girls, from all walks of life, to be and do what is pleasing in God's sight for the betterment of all.

I have received numerous requests to make my speeches and sermons available to people beyond my listening audience. For a long time, I resisted this alternative way of getting my words out; collecting them between covers seemed premature. But as the requests increased, I began to pray about it.

This book is an answered prayer. As the requests to collect my speeches and sermons kept coming, I realized that they were God's way of saying to me, "Here is your opportunity to get your speeches and sermons out to all people."

I have compiled and edited the speeches and sermons that I feel address the hard issues of our lives—about race, religion, family values, social and economic justice, and personal motivation. Some of them are tough in their content. Others are tender. If your life is comfortable, I hope you will be disturbed by my words, but if you are disturbed about life, I hope you will be comforted. However you are touched by the words that follow, may your journey through the following pages lead you to some heart answers.

PART ONE

DISTURBING

THE

COMFORTABLE

A
PROPHET
WITHOUT HONOR

everal years ago, President Reagan signed the legislation
setting aside the third Monday of January to celebrate
Martin Luther King Jr.'s birthday. Many across the land
rejoiced. For many of us, it was an honor long past due for a
man who changed the face of this nation. It was the first time
an African American was honored with a national holy day.
And now every January, in every state, we pause to honor the
man, the message, and his mission.

    Unfortunately, as we survey the land, we would have to
ask ourselves, where is the real honor? On the one hand, we
celebrate a man who stood for peace, and yet we are the most
violent nation in the world, so where is the real peace? We
pay tribute to a man who fought for justice, and yet we have
the Rodney King incidents. We pay tribute to a man who

Delivered at Ebenezer Baptist Church on January 18, 1993, to commemorate the twenty-fifth anniversary of the death of Martin L. King Jr.

fought for economic freedom, and yet African Americans are denied loans to buy homes and start businesses. We commemorate a man who struggled for equality, and yet African Americans continue to be judged first by the color of their skin and not by the content of their character. We honor a man who championed nonviolence, and yet we glorify violence from the silver screen to the TV screen, from the state house to the school house.

How dare we say we honor the life and legacy of Martin Luther King Jr. when we allow these atrocities to occur with impunity? We must do more than honor a man of this magnitude with just a holiday; we must honor him with action. We must honor him by bringing into reality what he merely dreamed about. Until we are willing to honor Dr. King with consistent, liberating actions, then we dishonor him with our mere words, and he is a prophet without honor.

Throughout history God has sent us prophets who have spoken the word, but who have seldom been heeded. In essence, they were forced to prophesy in a vacuum. That's why Jesus said, "A prophet is not without honor, save in his own country." (Matt. 13:57) It was, and in some cases still is, very difficult for America to find a real place for Martin Luther King Jr. We fear the prophet. We ridicule the prophet. We jail the prophet. We even kill the prophet. But we have no problem making the prophet merely a dreamer. Let's face it, there are some people in power who have no intention of allowing my dad's dream to become a reality.

I think that in order to understand what the Bible means, we must take a closer look at the role of the prophet. God has always found it in His divine order to visit us with prophets.

Prophets have always been God's instruments to change and help us reshape our lives. And just as God visited those of old, God visits us today. God sends us prophets who are not afraid to say, "Thus saith the Lord." Without a doubt, Martin Luther King Jr. was indeed a twentieth century prophet who came to his own, and his own received him not. Dr. King brought to us the breath of newness and vision we so desperately needed. It was because of his prophetic role that people were mobilized to the streets of Montgomery, Selma, and Birmingham in a movement for justice. It was because of his prophetic vision that those who had walked for years with their heads bowed down could now walk with a sense of respect, with their eyes to the hills from whence cometh their help. It was because of his prophetic vision that men who swept the streets gained courage to challenge the system and women who washed other people's clothes found faith to believe in themselves. It was because Dr. King allowed himself to be used by God that people laid down their egos, their ethnicity, their religion, and even their prejudices, and walked as one common humanity, with one common goal. The word of God is true, and it says, "Without a vision the people will perish." (Prov. 29:18)

We must pause today to ask the question, "Where is the prophetic vision?" Where are those who have not been bought with pseudo positions, and titles that they cannot spell, and positions that they cannot even pronounce? Where are those leaders who have not allowed themselves to be used by Pharaoh to continue the subtle enslavement of a people who have tasted the sweet savor of real freedom?

It is easy to honor a true prophet with words. We can talk

about what he did and how he changed America, and that is fine. But the real question is, "What am I doing?" We have seen the yearning to follow the prophetic message of Dr. King in South Africa, Haiti, Germany, Eastern Europe, and even in some places in America. But many are paying mere lip service to the name of Dr. King. We honor the name, but we do not adhere to the actions. We must face the fact that it is not enough to say, "We love Dr. King," "We respect Dr. King," "We honor Dr. King." In my mind, he would not be terribly impressed with our mere words and our lip service. He would say that you honor, love, and respect me by picking up where I left off.

My brothers and sisters, it is not enough to say that we marched with Dr. King twenty-five or even thirty years ago. We need to ask ourselves, what are we doing now? In fact, some of us have not truly marched in twenty-five or thirty years. How do we expect change to occur if we are not willing to put on the whole armor of God and fight injustice wherever it raises its ugly head?

Now, when Jesus said that "a prophet is without honor," He was really saying that we have a tendency not to appreciate people until they are dead. This is certainly our story because America has a serious disdain for live heroes and an affinity for dead ones. Elvis is still being sighted, and his stamp drew more people to Graceland than any one of his live concerts. It seems as long as we have them in the flesh, we have a tendency to take them for granted. Those who are more at a distance seem to be more appreciated and revered. But there seems to be an irony to it.

For you see, here we are twenty-five years after the death

of my father and thirty years after the "I Have a Dream" speech, yet where is the proper honor? We have a national holiday, and some people spend that day sitting around doing nothing. We ought to use this day to create and nurture greater racial understanding, friendship, and cooperation. For as my father said, "Like life, racial understanding is not something we find, but something that we must create . . . the ability to work together, understanding each other, will not be found ready made; it must be created by the fact of contact." We ought to use this day to teach our children self-respect—who they are, where they come from, how to love and help their neighbors. We ought to use this day to teach America that it is either nonviolence or nonexistence.

Those who walked with Dr. King say his contributions speak for themselves, and those who have come after say, "We respect the man, but his ideas are questionable, and his methodology is obsolete." This means that the further we move away from Dr. King and the civil rights movement the more we will need to teach future generations the true story. Without action, the forces of evil will continue to haunt us. Think about it.

It is no happenstance that there has been effort after effort to minimize and even to erase the contributions and accomplishments of Dr. King. Some have sought to promote him as a mere dreamer. Still others have subjected him to ill-suited comparisons. Others have sought to smear his image, and still others have dismissed his nonviolent philosophy as defunct and outdated. Many have misinterpreted his message and misunderstood his mission. But in spite of all these efforts, "We Shall Overcome" has been sung in Berlin, Soweto, Bosnia, Johannesburg, India, and Russia. They were able to kill the dreamer, but they will never kill the dream.

Dr. King said, "It is a dream deeply rooted in the American Dream." But I say to you that it is even bigger than that. It is a dream deeply rooted in what is noble, good, honest, respectful, and just. It is a dream that captures the very essence of the kingdom of God. It is for everyone, in every nation, in every time, from every religion, under every banner, for every just cause.

It was more than a dream, it was a prophetic vision, for Dr. King was a prophetic leader. He was prophetic when he said, "To ignore evil is to become an accomplice with it." When he spoke out against the Vietnam War, his prophetic voice was clear and unwavering. When he challenged the economic inequities that he saw and launched the poor people's campaign, he did not mince his words.

If we are going to carry out his prophetic message, then we need people and leaders who do not seek to just sit at Pharaoh's table, eat Pharaoh's foods, sip his wine and champagne, and get their minds off their mission. For you see, we can no longer be satisfied with just sitting at the table. It is time for us to start setting the menu. Many of us have been so elated that we have made it to the table, that until now we have not even been aware of what we have been eating. We have been eating the foods sacrificed to idol gods, the food of pride, conceit, power, racism, complacency, egoism, vanity, economic exploitation, and self-hatred.

It's time to wake up and see that the work of the prophet is not over. Sometimes a person has to put his life on the line. Sometimes a person has to point fingers, call names, uncover secrets, disclose double standards, call a spade a spade. Sometimes a prophet has to speak when no one is listening, go where no one will follow, and stand even when he is all alone.

When we look around at the nation's and the world's condition, I tell you, we need those who will heed Dr. King's words and example. For you see, the rich are getting richer and the poor are getting poorer. Our schools are failing us. Our economy is in shambles. Our government is corrupt. Drugs are rampant and kingpins rule the streets. You cannot convince me that we can send up space shuttles, satellites that have gone into black holes and taken pictures from light years away, and yet we don't have the capacity to stop the drugs from South America. I say to you it has nothing to do with our capacity; it has to do with our will. It has to do with our priorities.

We need people who can't be bought with money, position, or power. For you see, people are tired of leaders who are selling out. Some people get a little power and a little money and a little influence, and they lose all perspective. But we cannot condemn them. We have a responsibility to convert them. In the spirit of Dr. King, we must bring them back home and make them accountable.

We can best honor Dr. King by committing ourselves to those things for which he gave his life. He gave his life for justice for all people, democracy for all people, truth for all people, peace for all people, and love for all people.

So we cannot rest until justice means more than "just us" white folks. We cannot rest until health care is no longer a privilege for the rich and a curse for the poor. No one should rest until African Americans are adequately recognized for

9

the contributions they've made to this society. We cannot rest until our schools once again become places for learning and not battlegrounds for gang wars. We cannot rest until black men are no longer beaten by the new lynch mobs disguised in police uniforms. We cannot rest until the fighting ceases in Bosnia. We cannot rest until the fighting ceases in the Middle East and the Jews and Arabs sit down at the table of true brotherhood and sisterhood. We cannot rest until our children have a future where guns are not an everyday reality and the respect for human life is at the top of our agenda. If Dr. King and his prophetic role are to mean anything to us as we prepare to enter the twenty-first century, then we have got to stop playing games and get serious about building the kingdom of God.

When racism continues to raise its ugly head, somebody ought to do something. When almost 40 million Americans live in poverty, somebody ought to do something. When approximately 37 million have no health insurance, somebody ought to do something. When children are killing children in unprecedented numbers, somebody ought to do something. When African American students who attend majority-white institutions feel ignored and alienated because no one seems to care about their unique circumstances, somebody ought to do something. If we sit back and think that it's somebody else's problem, then some of us are going to be in for a rude awakening.

It's time for those of us who understand the message and mission of the prophet King to come together and make his spirit come alive again in our midst. Just as the disciples of Jesus were commissioned to spread the gospel of Christ, so,

jority." That's why he could translate "Love your enemies" into a life philosophy. That's why his rallying cry was "We wrestle not against flesh and blood, but against principalities, against powers." (Eph. 6:12)

Where do we go from here as the people of God? I suggest that we begin to make our lives and our society reflect the man we say we honor. This means we must acknowledge the fact that ours is a society bent on "mo'" money, "mo'" sex, and "mo'" violence. The sad part is that it's all based on the notion that this is what sells. But this kind of high-tech prostitution is why we're in the mess we're in today. No wonder our youth are rebelling. They are only embracing and mimicking what we're promoting. Gone are the days of saying, "Do as I say and not as I do." It's time to "train up a child in the way he should go" and go that way yourself. And that means we need to start doing those things that lead to a more sacred society.

Therefore, to truly honor Dr. King we need to feed the hungry, clothe the naked, visit those who are in prison, set the oppressed free, and proclaim the acceptable year of the Lord. Somewhere I read, "If you love Me, feed My sheep." "If you love Me, keep My commandments." "If you love Me, take up your cross and follow Me." "If you love Me, walk where I walk, and go where I lead you."

Dr. King certainly stood within the prophetic tradition. He took the word of God seriously. He loved God's people and sought to live out God's commandments. He told us, "The time is always ripe to do right," and like the historian Thomas Carlyle said, "No lie can live forever."

Well, the prophets of old denounced corruption, dishonesty, violence, cruelty, oppression, greed, arrogance, apathy, lust for power, and idolatry. The Lord said to Moses, "Go to Pharaoh and tell old Pharaoh to let My people go." The Lord said to Martin, "Go to Montgomery; go to Birmingham; go to Selma; go to Albany; go to Washington; tell old Pharaoh to let My people go."

Sanballat (Nehemiah's enemy) said, "Come here, Nehemiah. I know that you are rebuilding the wall. Come on down and let's pass some legislation. Come on down and let us hold some senate hearings. Come on down, Nehemiah, and let us get tough on crime and build more prisons." Nehemiah said, "I can't come down. Why should God's work cease while I come down to you? I can't come down."

God said, "Well, Isaiah, there is trouble in the land. Look up and tell me what you see." Isaiah said, "I saw also the Lord sitting upon the throne, high and lifted up, and his train filled the temple. Also I heard the voice of the Lord, saying, 'Whom shall I send, and who will go for us?' Then said I, 'Here am I; send me.' " (Isa. 6:1,8)

God said, "Well, Amos, what do you have to say about the situation?" Amos said simply, "Let justice roll down like waters, and righteousness like an everflowing stream." (Amos 5:24)

Then one day the Lord took a prophet by the name of Ezekiel and placed him in the midst of a valley of dry bones, and he asked the question, "Son of Man, can these bones live?" And Ezekiel looked at the bones, and they were very dry: violence in our cities, jails on the rise, schools unable to teach. They were very dry. South Africa in turmoil, babies having babies, homelessness on the rise. They were very dry. Deficit choking the economy. Trust at an all-time low. They were very dry. Can these bones live?

And then Ezekiel heard a voice say, "Prophesy to the bones." And Dr. King heard the same voice, and he began to speak. Soon, a foot bone from Frederick Douglass found an ankle bone from Harriet Tubman, and they connected with a leg bone from Nat Turner and a knee bone from Mary McLeod Bethune. A thigh bone from John Kennedy found a hip bone from Richard Allen. A back bone from Fannie Lou Hamer found a shoulder bone from Malcolm X. And a neck bone from Coretta Scott King found a head bone from Bennie Mays. Dr. King kept on prophesying—through the Kennedy era, the Johnson era, the Nixon era, the Ford era, the Carter era, the Reagan era, the Bush era, and the prophetic voice of Dr. King will continue to be heard during the Clinton era.

Stand up, prophets, cry out and proclaim the acceptable year of the Lord. When the dry bones come together, black and white, yellow, brown, and red; rich and poor; learned and unlearned; from Morehouse to no house; from Vanderbilt to the house that Jack built; from Los Angeles to Russia; from the Middle East to the Midwest; from Bosnia to Birmingham; from the New South Africa to New Hampshire; we shall usher in that day when justice will reign, democracy will prevail, and love will be a reality. Together, we shall overcome.

A little more than twenty-five years ago, when I was only five years old, my head lay on my mother's lap as we sat on the front pew of Ebenezer Baptist Church. It was the home-going service for my father. All of the people, all of the lights, all of the cameras—I didn't quite understand. I was bewildered, perplexed, confused.

April 1968 was an emotionally devastating time for many others as well. It was a time of pain, frustration, anger, bitterness, and ambivalence. The death of Martin Luther King Jr. left a void. We lost the man. We lost our brother. We lost our father. We lost the leader. We lost the prophet. "Why now?" we asked. "What do we do?" "Who will lead us to the promised land?"

A raging sea of doom and hopelessness consumed the land. The sun set, and it seemed as if there was no light to guide the people. But with every sunset, praise be to God, there's always a daybreak to follow. For, "Weeping may endure for a night, but joy cometh in the morning." (Ps. 30:5)

Now it's morning time. The alarm clock has already gone off, and we've worn out the snooze button. It's time to get up, turn off the alarm clock, and start a new day. Weeping time is over. And I don't know about you, but I'm tired of weeping. I'm tired of weeping over the murder of black boys. I'm tired of crying over the abuse of young children. I'm tired of weeping over the sexual exploitation of women. I'm tired of weeping about the economic exploitation of a powerless people. I'm tired of weeping over the inadequacies of an educational system. I'm tired of weeping over all the gun violence from out-of-control and angry people. I'm tired of weeping over racial arrogance and racial ignorance. Wake up, people. It's morning time. It may seem that we haven't gained much ground since we lost Dr. King, but we've made it this far by faith by leaning on the Lord.

And mother, I thank God for you because for many, once Daddy was gone you became that beacon of hope and tower of strength. In many ways, you kept so many from drowning in their tears of disillusionment. In the midst of the vicissitudes and challenges of life, you have ensured that Daddy's legacy of hope would abide. Your refusal to back down from all the criticism about creating the King center is why today we can celebrate the life and legacy of Dr. King and why America has not self-destructed. Thank God that you have kept the vision of the prophetic visionary before us.

And as we celebrate this twenty-fifth anniversary, I suppose we are all wondering what the next twenty-five years may bring. I don't know, but I do know that "time is filled with swift transition, Naught of earth unmoved can stand, Build your hopes on things eternal, Hold to God's unchanging hand! Trust in Him who will not leave you, Whatsoever years may bring; If by earthly friends forsaken, Still more closely to Him cling." Yes, "Trials dark on ev'ry hand, and we cannot understand, All the ways that God would lead us to that blessed Promised Land; But He'll guide us with His eye, and we'll follow till we die. For we'll understand it better by and by" (from *The New National Baptist Hymnal*).

OUR YOUTH:
OUR RESPONSIBILITY

The pride and treasure of our nation is our youth. Any nation that neglects the teaching and the upbringing of its youth is a nation on the decline. But if we are honest, then we must confess that we as a nation have lost control of our young people. Too many of our most cherished possessions are wandering aimlessly through life, with little thought about tomorrow.

An elderly woman said, "For those of you who are quick to criticize the younger generation, just don't you forget who raised them"—or better yet, who did not raise them. In the animal kingdom, adults take care of their young. Cats take care of kittens, chickens take care of chicks, bears take care of cubs, dogs take care of puppies. But many of us humans walk away from our responsibility as adults.

Our nation prides itself on being one of the strongest, if not the strongest and most progressive nation on the face of the earth. But how can we be when our children are bloodying our streets and slaughtering innocents? How can we be when we are more preoccupied with making a living than with making a life? How can we be when we think that our solution is building bigger and more secure jails to lock up our youth? This is merely a cover-up of our failure as adults to deal with the difficulties of raising children in this violent climate.

Whenever young people get caught up in drug addiction, sexual promiscuity, or misdirected violence, they are merely responding to the self-hatred that has been instilled in them. For you see, people who have no self-respect have no problem disrespecting others. People who have no self-respect have no problem carrying a gun to school. People who have no self-respect have no problem cursing out their elders and lying to get what they want.

Our children are smart. They listen not only to what we say, they watch what we do, and sometimes what we do speaks so loud that they cannot hear what we say. They see the contradictions, the hypocrisy, and the inconsistencies in our lives, in our talk as well as in our walk.

The problem is we underestimate most of our children. You know and I know that children today are much more aware than children were twenty years ago. Because of television and computers and technology, our children have the capacity to learn more and faster, and every day they are learning. Unfortunately, many of them are learning the wrong things. They are trying to drink their way to sobriety, steal their way to wealth, and lie their way to justice. They are in search of props, juice (slang for respect).

Let us face it. We have been too busy making excuses for

our children and not working on remedies. We have been busy criticizing and not giving enough time to molding character. To be brutally frank with you, we have fallen out of favor with our youth, and they simply don't trust anyone over thirty. That's reality, but that's not the end. We must never lose sight of our responsibility to our children. The word *responsibility* means "the ability to respond." The issue here, though, is not do we have the ability, but do we have the will? Do we possess the capacity to confront our own fears of our youth and to deal with issues straight up, without zigging to the left and zagging to the right? Or have we become so paralyzed by our fears that we don't know our children any more?

I believe that God holds each generation responsible for the one that comes after it. There was a time when the community, the school, and the church or synagogue worked hand in hand. We had the communal, the intellectual, and the spiritual all working together to create a whole human being.

We understand that all human beings have a mind, body, and soul regardless of their color, their religion, their creed, or their economic status. However, in the last three decades, we have caused a serious division in the human personality. We have raised a great number of young people who have no roots, little foundation, and virtually no spiritual guidance. We have created a welfare system that further dehumanizes and degrades.

I would be the first to say that there are some, though, who treasure the worth of the individual. I thank God that within the system there are a few brave soldiers who see these young children and young people not simply as some nebulous statistic, but as people with feelings, desires, hopes, and dreams just like everyone else. I thank God that there are people who have a burning desire to help and assist our young people, who understand that in most cases these young people are mere victims.

Victor Hugo, that great philosopher, once said, "Where there is darkness, sins will be committed. But he who is guilty is not only he who committed the crime, but he who created the darkness." It seems as if many of us have gone into a blame-the-victim syndrome. When all else has failed—when we have failed, when society has failed—blame the *victims*. It is easier this way.

All over the country there is talk about welfare reform, and I think most of us agree that the present welfare system has not worked. We have blamed the many for the fault of the few. Too often we focus on the mothers and forget about the innocent children in these circumstances. But thank God that there is always a ram in the bush. People and organizations that have become the saving grace for many of these innocent children who are victims of a failed welfare system.

We have a tendency to raise a lot of concerns and questions about single heads of households as if it were a new phenomenon. But we have always had single heads of households, and children did not turn out the way they are turning out today. Even I was raised by a single head of household. But there were certain things that I could do, and there were certain things that I better not do.

Today, in many households, it is not clear who is in charge. It seems in some cases that the children are raising the parents rather than the parents raising the children. And if we really wanted to be honest about it, children are raising children when they have never been parented themselves.

We teach children the alphabet. We teach them how to catch a ball. We teach them how to put on their clothes, but we don't teach them self-respect. We don't teach them values. We don't teach them how to honor their elders. And when children are not taught to honor those who have come before; when they are not taught to respect those who have paid the ultimate price; when they are not taught to revere those upon whose shoulders we stand, then why should we expect them to act civilized? Why should we expect them not to be disciplinary problems?

It is true, as the Bible says, that we reap what we sow. You cannot sow hatred and expect to reap love. You cannot sow ignorance and expect to reap wisdom. You cannot sow disrespect and expect to reap honor. You cannot sow cheating and expect to reap truth. It is a universal fact: "What goes around, comes around."

Admittedly, some of our children have problems. Some of them are very confused. They look at Watergate and Iran Contragate and S&L Gate and Senate Gate, they hear about elected officials caught with their hands in the cookie jar taking money from crooks, they see drugs and guns in their community and everybody trying to pass the buck, and they become confused. We confuse our children and then blame them for their confusion. This is irresponsible, reprehensible, and downright repugnant. Our children deserve better from us.

We live in a nation with approximately 23 million of our citizens functionally illiterate. Among mothers on welfare, one in three is illiterate. Approximately 37 million Americans have no health insurance. Yet, because of double standards, we continue to spiral down into a dungeon of despair and deception.

We say to our young people that we have little or no money for jobs, little or no money for training, little or no money for scholarships and grants, little or no money for housing. But we can find $500 billion to bail out the savings and loan crooks, and they are out of jail in two years. We can convict Oliver North for lying to the Congress and trans- gressing the law of the land, and now he makes around $25,000 a speech and was nearly elected to be a United States senator. Our children may not know all the names, but they do understand and comprehend all the blatant lies and con- tradictions. They know that they can't go to college while $150 million satellites get *lost in space!* My brothers and sis- ters, I submit to you that we underestimate the intelligence of many of our youth. They see the Academy Awards and the American Music Awards. They watch the videos, and some even look at "Lifestyles of the Rich and Famous," and they ask, "Why can't I have that?" They want the same things in life that other people want.

But theirs is a different world. Their world is filled with crack houses and drive-by shootings, with abuse and neglect, with crime and decay, with neglect and abandonment. Some- times even the police are afraid to enter into their world. But enter into their world we must. We have no choice but to lay down our fears and frustration and recapture the imagination of our youth. These are not some children from outer space, from some other planet. They are our sons and daughters. Our blood flows through their veins. Their destiny is tied to our destiny, and whoever they are, we made them; where they are, we brought them; and what they know, we taught them.

It is up to us to recapture their youthful fantasies and create for them a world that is hopeful and promising. The challenge is indeed an awesome one, but one that we must face head on. To run away is to destroy our own future.

Robert Kennedy once said, "Some men see things as they are and ask why. I dream things as they ought to be and ask, why not?" I thank God that there are some who refuse to believe that the present welfare system is not in need of reform. But we must be careful that we do not allow ourselves, in the frenzy of coming up with something, to neglect the very people the system is designed to serve.

Without a doubt, we have a corrupt system, and it is not only corrupt from the bottom up, it is also corrupt from the top down. We have allowed our government to waste billions of dollars. Many of us remain silent in the midst of this corruption.

Some will tell us to wait and not to rock the boat. But when the welfare and treatment of these children are our last priority, somebody ought to rise up and say enough is enough. Somebody needs to speak on behalf of that mother who is nothing more than a child herself. Teenage pregnancy is out of control. Why? Not just because our children just love sex, not just because they love to pull their pants down or their skirts up, not even because no one is at home, but simply because everybody wants to be loved.

Many in our society have bought into the myth that these young ladies just want to be on welfare. Admittedly, some do, but the overwhelming majority do not. It's not about receiving food stamps. It's not about getting a meager $287 a month and selling your dignity to the mailman. No!!! It's also about when your baby gets sick at night and needs a doctor—what hospital can you go to? I submit to you that the reason many mothers are on welfare is not the food stamps, not the check, *but the health care!!!*

Isn't a poor, scared, lost, welfare mother's child just as important as any other child? Shouldn't a three-month-old baby with meningitis be given the proper and best medical treatment, regardless of the economic status of his or her parents? I don't need to tell you that poor children are dying while children with health insurance are living. Just because this is the way it is does not mean that this is the way it ought to be. *Health care can never become a privilege for the rich and a curse for the poor.*

Whatever we might think of President Clinton's health care proposal, all American citizens deserve not to have to worry about their health. If France can provide health care for all its citizens, then why can't we? If Canada can do it, then why can't we? If the Russians can do it, then why can't we? Health should never be a privilege reserved only for the rich but a *right* of every American. We must begin to attack the problems holistically and stop this piecemeal, quilt-patching approach to health care that we have been employing for the past three decades.

Whose responsibility is it? It is yours and mine. Government will do no more than what we make government do.

The simple tragedy is that so many of us think that we have made it, when in reality we are just a couple of paychecks away from the welfare lines ourselves. You do not have to be born poor to end up poor. With the layoffs and cutbacks, we are now getting people with college degrees on welfare. We must do something, and we cannot wait.

A father and his son went fishing one day. While they were out on the lake, the little boy started giggling. The father asked, "What is so funny, Jimmy?" The little boy just kept on laughing. A short time later, little Jimmy started laughing again. Dad said, "Come on, Jimmy, tell me what is so funny." Little Jimmy pointed his finger under his Dad's feet and said, *"Dad, you're going to drown. You have a hole in your side of the boat."* Little Jimmy did not realize that he was in the same boat, and that if Dad was going to drown, then so was he. *Brothers and sisters, we may have come here on different ships, but we are all in the same boat now.* Black and white, rich and poor, northside and southside, learned and unlearned, we will either make it in together or ultimately drown in the sea of indifference.

What can we do for our young people? We have a responsibility to be role models for them, to show them that people can still be compassionate and caring. We must demonstrate to them that people can still look out for each other's children and that neighbors can talk to each other and know each other's name. We must say to our young people: "Do more than exist—*live.* Do more than touch—*feel.* Do more than look—*observe.* Do more than hear—*listen.* Do more than listen—*understand.* Do more than think—*ponder.* Do more than talk—*say something.*

Some of you may have heard about, and were startled by, the nineteen children found in a one-room apartment in Chicago. These children were sharing a chicken leg with the dog. The roaches had moved in as tenants, and the rats had become permanent fixtures. It was a deplorable and disturbing sight. How we would like to think that this was just an isolated case when we know in our hearts that it was not. Unfortunately, scenes like this occur everywhere in America. In Atlanta, Detroit, New York, Washington, D.C., Kansas City, in your hometown and my hometown, children have become like animals. But I know and my Bible tells me that we were created just a little bit lower than the angels.

Yes, we are living below our potential. We are not fulfilling the greatness that is in each of us. We are not calling forth the best that our children have to offer. We allow them to get by with doing just enough to satisfy the grade. We label them slow learners—"learning disabled," "functionally deprived," "educably defunct"—and our labels contribute to their demise.

It is not enough for us to just talk the talk. We must be willing to walk the walk. We must be able to stand in front of our children and remind them that in their veins flows the blood of kings and queens, doctors and astronomers. In their veins flows the blood of Frederick Douglass, Sojourner Truth, Harriet Tubman, Abraham Lincoln, John Fitzgerald Kennedy, Rosa Parks, Paul Robeson, James Baldwin, John Brown, Malcolm X, Coretta Scott King, Carolyn Mosely Brown, Barbara Jordan, Dorothy Day, and Martin Luther King Jr. And it is not enough for them to just know that; they must commit themselves to live that. They must know that to live below one's potential is to rob oneself of one's future. We must teach them that "vacant minds and vacant lots usually become dumping grounds for junk."

Dr. Benjamin Elijah Mays, the now-deceased, past president of Morehouse College, once said, "Nobody is wise enough, nobody is good enough, and nobody cares enough about you for you to turn over to them your future and your destiny." We must teach our children that life is more than more prestige and more power. Life is also making a constructive difference in somebody's life. You are in a position to make that constructive difference.

I have come to realize that it is not where you come from that really matters; it is where you are going. Where are we going as a people? How important are our children to us? Raising our children must become a top priority in our lives. Cultivating their minds, strengthening their bodies, and elevating their spirits ought to be uppermost on our agenda.

We must teach our children, as Horace Mann said, to "seek not greatness, but seek truth, and you will find both." We must teach our young people to

> Take time to work—it is the price of success
> Take time to think—it is the source of power
> Take time to play—it is the secret of perpetual youth
> Take time to read—it is the foundation of wisdom
> Take time to worship—it is the highway to reverence
> Take time to dream—it is hitching one's wagon to a
>   star
> Take time for friendship—it is a source of happiness
> Take time for God—it is life's only lasting investment

Now is the time to take time. Now is the time to put up or shut up. Now is the time.

FREEDOM FROM VIOLENCE:
A VISION FOR FAMILIES
AND COMMUNITIES

Our society has lost its sense of mission and purpose, and in so doing we have neglected the basics that make life worth living. We have become preoccupied with the trivial and the mundane and have refused to face the hard realities of human existence. This has created a criminal justice system that is overburdened and inept. This is not an indictment upon any one individual, but upon our society as a whole.

I firmly believe that if we are going to change the present chaotic situation we find ourselves in, then we need to do some serious examinations of ourselves and our institutions. We have to begin asking ourselves some heart-searching questions.

Why is it that thirty to forty years ago we as a nation did not experience the level of violence that we are now experiencing? Or, for that matter, fifteen to twenty years ago? What is the correlation between our failure in education and rising crime statistics? Is there a relationship between unemployment, a failed educational system, and the rising tide in youth violence?

The answers to these questions seem rather obvious. We all know the answers, but we also know the causes. For too long those in the criminal justice system have focused on the symptoms and not the causes. It seems that every institution in our society wants to blame some other institution and in the meantime, our young people are killing each other and our communities are turning into battle zones.

Let's face it, brothers and sisters, violence has gotten out of hand, and with all our great minds, we really don't know how to deal with it. We ignored all the early warning signs, such as rising unemployment, teenage dropouts, teenage pregnancies, escalating poverty, a failed educational system, social policy shifts, and political insensitivity. And then when we did not know what to do, we started blaming the victims. We are still doing that, and the clearest indicator that we are is our juvenile criminal justice system. We have decided to lock up our children, treat them like adults, and throw away the keys.

Brothers and sisters, these are our children, they are not from Mars; they are not aliens, although they might act like it from time to time. These are our children, our responsibility, and somewhere we have failed them. Our schools have failed, our businesses have failed, our legal system has failed, our churches and synagogues and mosques have failed them, and in so doing we have turned them against us, against society.

Now, I would be the first to admit that a society cannot operate without law and order. But I would further submit to you that a society that addresses its problems strictly through law and order is a society that is on the verge of internal destruction. When we become so frustrated with ourselves that we would spend more money to lock up a person than we would spend to educate and train that same person, then we can no longer call ourselves a progressive and civilized nation.

Youth violence is real. However, we must understand that the behavior is a symptom, not the cause. Until we begin to address the causes we will be building more jails and locking up more of our children. But this has not and will not stop the violence because what is lacking is the moral fortitude, the moral will.

If we were honest, we would have to admit that we are morally bankrupt. We are value depleted, we are integrity depleted, impoverished morally, and we do not value human life. Our people watch junk all day long on the television. They listen to junk all day long on the radio. They read junk all day long in the papers. What do we expect? Junk on top of junk leads to junk, every day of the week. By the same token, value on top of value leads to value, all day long. I'm not talking about conservative or liberal values. I'm talking about human values, respect for life, respect for elders, respect for self, hard work, courtesy, honesty, and obeying the law. A major part of our problem is partisan politics that put expediency above principle, that place favoritism above moral correctness. I believe that we have made the criminal justice system into *big business*. We have so institutionalized our handling of deviate behavior, and so specified every conceivable

31

•

discipline, that a lot of people would be out of work if we actually solved the problem. Therefore, we perpetuate the system rather than alleviate the problem.

How do we then begin to seriously and sincerely address this problem of violence? *First,* we must admit that what we have tried has failed. This is not to cast blame upon anyone or any group. It is merely to state a fact: we have failed. If our efforts and theories and laws had worked, then we would not have to discuss the issue. We have been working *at* the problem rather than *on* the problem.

I realize it is very difficult for a professional people, a well-trained people, a very qualified people, a hard-working people, a proposal-writing people, to face up to the hard reality that what we have come up with thus far just has not worked. It does not mean that you or I are any less of a person; it simply means that the problem is bigger than us and that we alone are not going to solve it.

Admitting failure can be a healthy thing if approached properly. It can be employed as a tool for growth and renewal. Failure can be a doorway to opportunity. Failure is merely an indicator that somebody had the guts to try. You know, many of us are so wrapped up in being successful in our chosen professions that we never stop to think, "Successful by whose definition?" Much of what we consider successful now is antiquated, obsolete, and irrelevant. We define ourselves by the standard that has been set by others rather than by the ideas of who we ought be and are capable of becoming.

In essence, in our professional and legal lives we have lost our ability to dream. We go along to get along because that is what the profession demands of us. We are told and believe that if you want to make it, you conform, you adjust, you fit in. You find a way to integrate, to be accepted, not to rock the boat.

Well, while we have been doing this, our children have been dying, and our communities have become wastelands. Why? Because we refuse to own up to the fact that however noble our intentions, however honorable our aspirations, the problems have gotten worse.

It is not just the legal profession that has failed. It is the educational, the political, the economic, the social systems and even the religious profession that have failed. And in our failure, we have allowed those who perpetuate violence, and make big money off of violence, to run rampant. Facing this hard reality is the first step toward a community free from violence and racism, and sexism and militarism; a community where laws are minimal and respect is maximal; a community where violence is a thing of the past; a community where our children grow up in a healthy environment and people look out for each other. But in order to achieve this, we must first admit that we have failed, and we have failed because our aim has been low.

Second, we must build bridges and relationships with other disciplines. Part of our problem in this society is simply that we do not talk to each other. We each get only a fragment of the problem, and we conduct ourselves as if we have the whole thing. There has been just too much separation among the various disciplines it takes to make a child whole.

When was the last time DAs, public defenders, judges, ministers, politicians, educators, business persons, social scientists, and community activists sat down to focus on the solution and not the problem? When was the last time we sought to develop a collective agenda, a plan of action, an attack, if you will, on the causes of violence?

In our specialties, we have neglected to see the whole and have focused on just our element of the problem. Perhaps you have solved your part, but if the parent has not done his or her part, or if the teacher or the religious leader has not done his or her part, then we still have a big problem.

Instead of seeking to relate more and more to people in our own disciplines, which is far more comfortable, easier to manage, and thereby easier to control, we must seek means and ways of relating to people in other disciplines who share the same vision. The only real vision is a collective vision. Anything short of a collective vision is myopia. The real tragedy is that we focus on our element of the problem and address it with all of the best intentions and proper motives, but we come from a very limited perspective.

We need, our families need, and our children need people who are not afraid to wrestle with, confront, dialogue with, challenge, converse with, strategize with, and empathize with those who are different—those who may come with a different perspective, a different viewpoint, even a different starting point.

No longer can we afford to wait until every *t* has been crossed and every *i* has been dotted before we move. My father talked quite a bit about the "paralysis of the analysis"— how some people will study a problem to death instead of getting out there and taking some risk. With violence destroying our families the way it is now, we must be willing to take some risk and make some new enemies as well as some new friends. For if you don't risk, you won't grow, and without growth, death awaits you in the shadow of life.

Yes, if we are going to tackle at least some of the critical issues surrounding the violence in our society, then we must put forth a conscious, concerted effort to build new bridges. Once we understand that our reputation matters little, we can then move forward. Your reputation is what people think you to be; your character is what God made you to be. It's time to concern ourselves with character, not reputation. Bridge building and interdisciplinary dialogue is a part of the solution.

Let's face it, though: most people in our society are afraid to rock the boat. But I am afraid that if someone does not step forward and bring into being a new approach, a more courageous approach, a more disciplined approach, then there won't be a boat to rock.

Part of the problem is that we have deceived ourselves into thinking that we have arrived, that we have made it. But it does not matter what your station in life is, nor how much money you have acquired; none of us is immune to violence. It touches every social class, every economic division, every town and every city, and if it hasn't touched your family yet, it is, perhaps, just around the corner. Violence is our problem, and regretfully I submit to you that three strikes and you are out is not the answer, for just how many people are we willing to lock up? How many billions of dollars on jails are we willing to spend, while the problem continues to grow?

Our great nation has more than 4.4 million of its citizens, or almost 2 percent of the U.S. population, under some form of criminal justice control (including prisons, jails, probation, or parole). In fact there are thirteen states with a smaller pop-

35

ulation than the number of people who are incarcerated in jails and prisons. Another way of looking at it is that the number of people in our prisons and jails would comprise the eleventh largest city in America. We've got to go another way. This route has failed, is failing, and is doomed to fail.

Yes, we must admit our failures, and second, we must build coalitions, but *third,* we must attack poverty and racism because these two cohorts are the true culprits in domestic and family violence. We can either continue to pass the buck or we can take on these deadly evils. It would not be difficult to pass the buck because we already spend more money to incarcerate than we spend to educate. It makes one wonder, do we as a people really want to solve the issues of violence? I believe that with hard work and focus, we can get back there again.

Too many of our children are born out of wedlock; too many are raised in poverty; too many die too young. Over one-third of all African American children are born and raised in poverty, and we wonder why our jails are filled? We can no longer afford to postpone the response to this dilemma. The time is over for following our course of deception; we must seek truth at all cost, because it is the truth that will set us free. These young children become adults and they seek to survive by any means necessary.

The truth is that one out of every two black men will be arrested in his lifetime; and it's not all based on committing a crime. Some of it's based on just being a black man in the wrong place or right place but at the wrong time. One out of every four black men are under some form of criminal justice control. It is a fact that a black person in America is 7.4 times more likely to be imprisoned than a white person.

My brothers and sisters, it does not take a genius to figure out that racial discrimination plus poverty equals violence and crime, which translate into imprisonment and time. Is this the way we want our nation to continue to go? Are we going to choose to live in our fears for the rest of our lives? Or are we going to break away from the norm, and try a new thing, and live in our faith in humanity?

We must employ our legal mind to ensure that the nation moves forward. We must accept the fact that with all the laws on the books, with all the police on the streets, with more and more jails going up every day in our cities, we have not deterred crime. In fact, quite the contrary has occurred: crime has increased. Someone or *someones* need to say, wait a minute—this thing is costing too much money, and we are getting few results. If we were a corporation, we would have been bankrupt a long time ago. And if there is one thing that people understand, it's money.

Every new law is costing the taxpayer; every new jail is costing middle class America. Every miseducated, misguided child is jeopardizing the future of our nation.

The conflict is not between the old way and the new; the conflict is between the false way and the true. For any organization, program, agenda to move forward, it must have a vision. There must exist some ideal of what we are striving to achieve—something in which we are willing to invest our time, our energy, and our future. There are many organizations, and even governments, with no real vision. They have nice sounding words and beautifully outlined programs, but that does not mean that they have a vision.

Henry Ford had a vision about the automobile; the Wright

brothers had a vision about the airplane; Dr. Charles Drew had a vision about the Red Cross; Thomas Jefferson had a vision about the Constitution; NASA had a vision about space travel; Nelson Mandela has a vision for a new South Africa. What is our vision? What is *your* vision? To go along to get along? Or to use your creative matter for the betterment of our judicial system, for the betterment of every American, regardless of race, creed, color, religion, or political party?

Visions are important because they call us beyond ourselves; they call for the best in each of us. Now we must work together to create a new agenda, a new hope, a new challenge, and a new vision. Imagine a society with no guns, no weapons of any kind, no domestic or family violence. Imagine a people who love life, respect human beings, and appreciate the value of interaction. Imagine a society where politicians do not make promises they cannot keep, and presidents don't promise never to raise your taxes. Imagine a world where television teaches cooperation and conflict resolution, not confrontation. Imagine a world where lawyers, DAs, public defenders, judges, and preachers sit side by side to assist a young man in trouble.

One day as I was flying over the New York harbor, I looked at the Statue of Liberty, and was surprised when Lady Liberty winked at me. I waved at her and she smiled back. But then I noticed a strange look on her face. A look of someone in pain, someone in tremendous travail. I couldn't understand. I read her inscription: GIVE ME YOUR TIRED, YOUR POOR, YOUR HUDDLED MASSES YEARNING TO BREATHE FREE. Then I understood. The elderly, the unemployed, the disabled, the incarcerated, the young, the gang member.

In her hand was a copy of crime legislation that talked about more money for jails and police on the streets and three strikes and you're out.

I looked at the Statue of Liberty, and a tear streamed down her cheek. She sat down with her head locked in her shoulders and her torch hanging at her side. But then I heard the voices of DAs and judges from Georgia connecting with DAs from Florida connecting with DAs in Ohio at a national DAs' conference on youth violence in America. And they had in their hands a commitment letter to do all that they could to stop the violence and to stop the killings, to restore dignity and self-respect, and to stand on the premise that all persons are created equal and that they are endowed by the Creator with certain unalienable rights, and among these are life, liberty, and the pursuit of happiness.

Lady Liberty stood up, held high her torch, wiped away her tears, waved at all the advocates and DAs, gave out a great yell, and said, "We're on the move now." No fire can consume us; no water can wash us away; no veto can stop us; no budget cuts can hinder us; no state legislatures can dissuade us; and no fear will dominate us. God is on our side, and if God is for us, then who can be against us? Let us move forward to redirect our energies and to recapture and redirect our youth.

THE
DEATH PENALTY:
A MURDER VICTIM'S
PERSPECTIVE

Having lost my father and grandmother to gun violence, I well understand the deep hurt and anger felt by the loved ones of those who have been murdered. Yet I can't accept the judgement that their killers deserve to be executed. This merely perpetuates the tragic, unending cycle of violence that destroys our hope for a decent society.

I sometimes struggle with my own anger and negative feelings toward those who killed my father. He was a Christian minister who was assassinated while practicing the social gospel of service to the destitute. I remember my father saying, "I plan to stand by nonviolence because I have found it to be a philosophy of life that regulates not only my dealings in the struggle for racial justice but also my dealings with people, with my own self."

Then I remember that my beloved grandmother was slain while playing the organ in church, and that even after her death, my grandfather said, "I don't hate anybody." Both my father and my grandmother dedicated their lives to carrying forward the unfinished work of Jesus Christ, the Prophet and Savior who said we must turn the other cheek, put up our swords, and love and pray for our enemies and those who would abuse us.

This journey to genuine forgiveness, this journey of hope, has been a difficult pilgrimage for me, but I feel that I have finally crossed over. Today I understand that the need for revenge and the anger that accompanies it are sicknesses of the soul that ultimately destroy the one who harbors them.

Those who thirst for revenge may experience the illusion of satisfaction, but this never lasts long in people of conscience because every act of violence leaves in its wake the seeds of more violence. We don't redeem the loss of our loved ones by adding to the misery of our society and the callousness of our government. In the short term, the death penalty may satisfy the very human impulse to seek revenge. In the long run, however, compounding acts of brutality adds to the suffering of the loved ones of offenders and victims alike.

Revenge and retribution can never produce genuine healing. They can only deprive survivors of the opportunity for forgiveness and reconciliation that is needed for the healing process. Somehow, some way, we have to make something positive come out of tragedy, and we can't do this if we try to right the wrong of violence with more violence.

There came a time in my heart when I realized that if I was going to be true to my faith, I had to find a way to forgive James Earl Ray and Marcus Wayne Chenault, the man who killed my grandmother. As an ordained Christian minister, I have an even more compelling obligation to recognize them as my brothers. I have to love the evil-doers even as I deplore their deeds. This isn't easy, but the alternative is bitterness and anger for everyone involved.

The Christian religion strongly emphasizes the importance of forgiving in order to attain spiritual wholeness. I know that those who support the death penalty say there is scripture in the holy books of all religions, the New Testament included, that justifies retaliation. But you can also find mandates for forgiveness in the scriptures of all faiths. In all religions, we make a choice about what we emphasize, and I choose to come down on the side of a loving God with my Hindu, Muslim, Jewish, Buddhist, and Animist brothers and sisters who share this belief.

So I have personal reasons for opposing the death penalty, but as a concerned citizen, I have equally compelling social reasons to stand firm against state-sanctioned murder.

First, the death rows of America all have inmates who insist that they were wrongly convicted. The record suggests that some of them are telling the truth. It happens more often than we know or would like to admit. At least twenty-five Americans whose innocence was later revealed have been executed in this century. That's twenty-five innocent people slaughtered by our government. On the average, an innocent person has been convicted of murder in the United States once every year since 1910. Since 1972, the record shows that at least thirty individuals have been sentenced to death and later found to be innocent.

There is no getting around the evidence that innocent people are threatened by capital punishment. The death penalty makes irrevocable any possible miscarriage of justice. Even the execution of guilty persons is little comfort when the innocent are wrongly convicted and executed.

The death penalty is also racist in its application. Academic studies tell us that those convicted of capital crimes, regardless of their race, are up to thirty-three times more likely to be executed when the victim is white than when the victim in black. In fact, one would be hard pressed to find even one case in which a white person was executed after being convicted of killing a black person.

State-sponsored executions set a dehumanizing example of brutality that only encourages violence throughout society. Allowing the state to kill its own citizens for any reason diminishes our humanity and sets a dangerous and sadistic precedent that is unworthy of a civilized society. Every execution makes our state and local governments a little less humane, a little more willing to take human life, and pushes us a step backward from achieving a peaceful society in which we can all take pride.

At present, at least thirty-six states permit the death penalty. Ten of them even allow the execution of pregnant women. More than 1,900 prisoners are currently under death sentences in these states. Not all of them are guilty. Is it worth killing even one innocent person to execute 1,899 guilty people? If the answer is yes, then we are a long way from saying we have a just society.

One of the most frequently cited arguments supporting the death penalty is that it has a deterrent effect. But states that have reinstated the death penalty after abolishing it have not experienced a decline in criminal homicides.

If we are really interested in deterring homicides, there is one proven deterrent—handgun control. Wherever handguns have been restricted, human lives have been saved. In

1976, Washington, D.C., passed a freeze on handgun pur-
chases resulting in 25 percent fewer firearm homicides per
year and a 23 percent decrease in firearm suicides during the
next eleven years. During this period, handgun deaths remained constant in nearby counties in Virginia and Maryland.

In 1990, about twenty-four thousand Americans were
killed by handguns, including victims of homicides, accidents,
and suicides. In 1990, Japan, with about half the population of
the United States, had only eighty-seven handgun homicides,
according to the Washington office of Interpol. Great Britain,
with about a quarter of our population, had a total of twenty-
two handgun homicides. Canada, Sweden, and West Germany
all had well under a hundred handgun homicides in 1990
(Handgun Control, Inc., derived from FBI Uniform Crime
Reports). Why is there such a drastic difference in the number
of handgun homicides in other industrialized nations? Unlike
in the United States, in these nations handguns are so strin-
gently controlled that they are effectively banned. These statistics make it clear that stronger handgun control measures
would be a far more effective deterrent to homicide in the
United States than capital punishment has ever proven to be.

Another reform that must be adopted if we are to put a
stop to the murder epidemic that is destroying our cities is to
take a stronger stand against the glorification of violence in
American films, television, and popular music. Every year
there are literally hundreds of incidents of violence by young
people who are copying acts of violence they have seen in a
movie or on television.

Now, I'm not advocating censorship by law, although I
think we need more warning label advisories and a different

rating system. We have to get organized as citizens and as consumers and create some accountability for banks and financial institutions that support slasher films and other forms of media that glorify violence. We have to become more active about confronting the culture of violence that permeates American media, including consumer boycotts, if necessary. We have to find new ways of encouraging and challenging them to sponsor art and entertainment that celebrate peace and love and create a culture of nonviolence.

Another mistaken belief about the death penalty is that it saves taxpayers the cost of supporting a prisoner for life. In reality, there is strong evidence that executions are even more expensive than incarceration. In 1982, for example, the average cost of a capital offense trial in New York, through the first stage of appeals alone, was about $1.8 million, more than twice the expense of life imprisonment.

The community of nations that have abolished the death penalty now includes France, Germany, Sweden, Australia, Denmark, Costa Rica, Venezuela, Austria, the Netherlands, Nicaragua, Norway, the Philippines, and the new nation of Namibia. Other countries, like Great Britain, Israel, and New Zealand, have capital punishment only for "exceptional crimes," like high treason. Of all the industrialized nations, only the United States and South Africa subject their citizens to capital punishment as an acceptable form of punishment. Furthermore, the United States is the only nation that allows execution by gas, electrocution, and lethal injection. If the United States is ever going to be credible as a moral world leader, though, we are going to have to abolish the death penalty.

However, that should not discourage us in any way from

working toward this goal. It just means we are going to have to work harder to educate people about the true effect of the death penalty. Every journey begins with one step. My father often said that it is not always popular to be right, but that's what moral leadership is all about—setting a higher standard of courage, compassion, and justice. He went on to say that "The ultimate measure of a person is not where he stands in moments of comfort and convenience but where he stands at times of challenge and controversy."

So I salute all of those who, as Saint Paul suggested, have "put away childish things" like revenge and retaliation. I salute those who, through bravery and decency, have worked against this controversial injustice. Your journey is truly a journey of hope, and I think the loved ones you have lost to the violence in our society would be very proud of the stand you are taking to create a more nonviolent society.

These efforts will one day reap a great victory for all humanity. The suffering and sacrifice that many of us have endured because of our loved ones who have paid the highest price will surely be redeemed in a more just and loving America for all of our children and their children to come.

Our magnificent example of love and forgiveness will one day prove irresistible to all people of goodwill everywhere. As time does and will reveal, forgiveness is a creative, transforming, healing force that breaks the cycle of violence and lights the way to the great community of brotherhood and sisterhood that is our highest calling.

RECOVERING
OUR TRUE IDENTITY BY
BREAKING DOWN DIVISIONS

P robably the most prominent issue of our time is race relations. On the one hand, we promote ourselves as one nation under God, indivisible with liberty and justice for all. On the other hand, our daily existence suggests that we are a nation divided between the blacks and the whites, the haves and the have-nots, the North and the South, the hip-hop culture and the traditional mainstream cultures, the conservatives and the liberals. Without a doubt, however, it is our racial division that is most difficult to shake off. It is an American dilemma. One hundred thirty years after the Emancipation Proclamation, twenty-nine years after the Civil Rights Act, and thirty-nine years after *Brown v. the Board of Education,* racism, separatism, and segregation are still the rule, not the exception. The Jim Crow–era signs are gone, but they are etched in the hearts and minds of men and women. Why do you think that many of the public school systems in our nation are majority black, while most private schools are primarily white? Why are black men locked behind jail bars, while a white man who commits the same crime is usually given a lesser sentence, placed on probation, or let off? Why is a neighborhood still viewed as a "black neighborhood" or a "white neighborhood"? Why are most corporate executives primarily WASP (white Anglo-Saxon Protestant) males? Why doesn't the educational curriculum from prekindergarten through postgraduate reflect the contributions to American culture made by African Americans, Native Americans, and other ethnic groups? These disheartening facts result from our national obsession with racial division.

It was W. E. B. DuBois who said, "The problem in the twentieth century is the problem of the color line" *(The Souls of Black Folk,* 1903). It is a fact that America is a racist nation. Whether we like it or not, whether we agree with it or not, most of us are caught up in an identity crisis dictated by race. For blacks, it has been a history of trying to find an appropriate sense of somebodiness, an appropriate name for ourselves to embrace. First we were Coloreds, then during the Jim Crow days we were referred to as Negroes. Then the black power movement awakened us to the reality of our blackness; since then black has become the acceptable term of reference. Then we got comfortable with finally being Americans, but with increased awareness that our cultural heritage is tied to Africa; we now refer to ourselves as African American (used interchangeably with black). We suffer from an identity crisis, but we are not alone. Why is it that we have groups like the Aryan Nation, the skinheads, and the Freemen? These organizations embrace the irrational beliefs that white is superior and that whites should not mix with other races. And why is it that as soon as the sun is shining, you can look around the pool or on any beach and find whites trying to get a sun-tan? This race thing has really gotten the best of us.

If we journey through that ancient document that defines our Judeo-Christian heritage, the Bible, we discover that race is really a human phenomenon. In the entire Bible, there is not a single reference to race as a way of identifying a group of people. In fact, Genesis 10:32 tells us that after God flooded the earth He divided the families of the sons of Noah into nations (Noah, his wife, three sons, and their wives were the only humans spared life as a result of the flood). It was through Noah's sons—Ham, Shem, and Japheth—that the earth became populated. This means all of us are descendants of Noah through Ham, Shem, or Japheth, that, ultimately, we are all related. This is what Paul meant when he said, "He has made from one blood every nation." (Acts 17:26) It is no concern to God whether we are black, white, red, yellow, or brown. God is calling nations of people, not races, to repentance. This fact is reflected in Jesus' great commission to his disciples, "Go ye therefore, and teach [not races, but] all nations." (Matt. 28:19) What does this mean for us in America? It means that God will not be pleased with us until we rise above our race problems and begin coexisting as a nation of people.

The fact that on any given Sunday morning, most worship services are thoroughly segregated would suggest that even the custodians of our religious heritage are caught up in divisions. How ironic, considering that we worship a God who is a spirit, which means that God is beyond what we see with our visible eyes—culture, ethnicity, or race. Therefore, until

49

the church of God gets together to break down the fleshly things that divide us, it will be difficult to heal our communities, cities, and nation from divisiveness.

The story of the day of Pentecost in Acts 2 is about breaking down barriers. Pentecost drew Jews and Galileans to Jerusalem—Jews for their annual festival of weeks (a festival of thanksgiving for the harvested crops), and Galileans who were waiting for the promise of the outpouring of Jesus' spirit. When the Holy Spirit descended upon the Galileans on the day of Pentecost, they began to speak the various languages and dialects of the Jews gathered in Jerusalem that day. The Jews were caught off guard because they couldn't understand how Galileans could speak their language. The Jews had gotten caught up in those fleshly concerns of culture, language, ethnicity, and religion. But God was seeking to do a new thing through the Galileans. He was breaking down those barriers that separated people by culture, language, ethnicity, race, or religion. It was not about the Jew or the Gentile. It was about all who opened themselves up to receiving the power of the Holy Spirit to do the will of God. Whatever the forces that previously divided the Galileans and the Jews, on the day of Pentecost a new relationship was formed between the two because, we are told, three thousand souls (persons not races) were saved that day, and all were with one accord.

As people of God, we need to operate in the Spirit of God to break down the barriers that divide us. The world is waiting for the church to come together in unity and be like the church in Acts, being with one accord. Unfortunately, though, many of us have become burdened by social distinctions. God did create us male and female, of different ethnicities, from different places, in different socio-economic classes, with different religions, but He intended for us to use these distinctions in ways that are positive and reaffirming rather than negative and demeaning. When we allow distinctions to become barriers we prevent the work of God from being done. The church is too paralyzed by what I call interdenominational and intradenominational prejudice. The Pentecostals say the Methodists are not sufficiently spirit-filled. The Methodists say the Baptists are too emotional. The Baptists say the Presbyterians are too intellectual. It is a most difficult proposition to get churches to come together. Protestants don't want to work with Catholics. Jews don't want to work with Muslims. We even find that one Baptist church hesitates to work with another Baptist church. But it's a sad day when the people of God won't come together to do the will of God.

Before the world can move beyond classism, sexism, territorialism, racism, then the church will have to move beyond religionism. When we allow ourselves to operate in the spirit of God, we know that there is no such thing as "I'm better than you," and we end up focusing on our similarities rather than our differences. When we let go and let God, we will realize that in spite of what makes us different we are all created in the image of God. So when we create a division between ourselves and others based on race, ethnicity, or religion, we must remember that these divisions are not created by God but are created in the minds and thoughts of people. When we submit to the spirit of God, it moves around our classism, knocks down our sexism, climbs over our racism, and pushes aside our religionism.

Therefore, as the church of God, we should not see ourselves as divided factions and sectarian groups with our own agenda and purpose, but rather as a unified force called out to do the will of God. It is time for the church of God, old and young, rich and poor, black and white, to come together. Too many Americans are outside the arc of safety for us to be preoccupied with our racial, religious, and other distinctions. Jesus said, "Whoever does the will of God is my brother, and sister, and mother." (Mark 3:35) Therefore, our brothers and sisters are those who do the will of our Father, not because they are black or white, not because they go to the same church. We've got to look beyond our affiliation to a particular church or our allegiance to a particular race. My father, Martin Luther King Jr., often said that we are tied in an inescapable network of mutuality, a single garment of destiny, and that what affects one directly affects all indirectly. We need to see ourselves as interrelated, as connected, as raised up and called out to break those strongholds that have divided us and crippled us and blurred the vision that God has given to this nation. We are an army of God, warriors called out to do the will of God. The only thing that makes us physically different from our next brother or sister is melanin, the chemical in our bodies that determines our complexion, giving us a darker skin tone if we have a lot of it and a lighter skin tone if we only have a little.

We must do more, then, than just teach an Afrocentric or Eurocentric or Asiacentric gospel. No, we are all children of Noah by descent, children of Abraham by faith. We are all created in the image of God. Our outward appearance, culture, and race are not what saves us. The world would have us believe that these outward designations are most important, but we cannot think like the world. Yes, we each have a homeland, but we are all Americans. I'm an American of African descent. My culture, my nationality, is that of American or black or African American. My identity is in Christ Jesus, through whom I have been made free.

When we truly embrace our spiritual identity, what we see with our eyes and hear with our ears won't matter. The kind of clothes we wear, the type of car we drive, the language we speak will be of no consequence. When we operate in our spiritual identity, we will see God in other people. It is Christ in us that saves us, not the black, red, brown, yellow, or white skin, not the male or female gender. As inheritors of the promise through Abraham, we should recognize that the word of God does not speak to our race or our gender but to our hearts, souls, minds, and spirits. Therefore, neither the degree of melanin in our skin nor the scars of our racial history should prevent us from doing God's work.

Before we can do it effectively, though, we must be willing to deal realistically with our race problem. The fact is, we are too race-conscious in this nation. The reason it is often difficult for blacks to get beyond accusing whites of racism is because race is so often an undertone in the way other races treat blacks. Almost invariably a black man, unless he has on a suit or tie, cannot shop without being followed around the store by a suspicious shopkeeper, who is usually non-black. Non-blacks often refer to blacks as "you people." The classic case of racism is when blacks move into a white neighborhood or community, and crosses are burned in their yards or there is a mass white exodus from the area. These acts communicate whites' continuing discomfort with blacks.

Racism in America exists because the white community, as a whole, has made race a problem from generation to generation. In general, blacks don't have a problem with race. Blacks are used to being in the company of people of other races, particularly whites. Our bosses are white; the storeowner is white; the doctor is white; the teacher is white. So doing away with racism is ultimately the responsibility of the white community. The role and responsibility of the black community is to fight against feelings of inferiority that are created as a result of institutionalized racism.

What has happened, then, as a result of all of this racism is that the white person is carrying around a lot of guilt and fear that have affected his psyche and spirit, while the black person is carrying around a lot of anger and is unable to forgive whites. As a result, we are not free to relate to each other. Therefore, we as blacks have to free whites from their guilt and fear so they can have genuine relationships with us, based on the realization that we are all created in the image of God. On the other hand, we as blacks need whites to free us from our fear—the fear of being rejected because of our race, which is debilitating at the least. I believe that as soon as whites are willing to release us from our fear and blacks are willing to forgive, then we will be able to establish true relationships that are not based on trying to prove ourselves. I'm tired of having to be better than the best and faster than the rest. It's time for all of us to be freed from these cultural burdens. For in Christ there is neither Jew nor Greek, bond nor free, male nor female. We are all one in Christ Jesus.

Before we can heal America and take back our cities, we've got to get together in the body of Christ. We've got to be able to hug each other without fear of the color rubbing off on us. We've got to get rid of our fear that if someone of a different race marries our son or daughter it will diminish our family. As long as we are caught up in these fears, we are not free of racism or prejudice and, therefore, we are not free in our spirit to do the will of God.

When the apostle Paul told his brothers and sisters that nothing should be able to separate you from the love of God, through Christ Jesus, he was really saying that neither race nor religion, doctrine, ritual, nor culture should stop you from working together in service to God.

There was once a man who died and was visited by an angel. This angel took the man to a kingdom on one side of the universe, and there this man saw a huge banquet table with all the delicacies of life. There was fried chicken, collard greens, black-eyed peas, and cornbread. There was prime rib, baked potatoes, and green beans. There was even a salad bar for the vegetarians. The food was absolutely a delight to the palate. In fact, it was so good that your tongue would beat your brains out trying to get to it. But the man noticed something strange. The people were frail; there was no laughter, no joy, little mobility. And he asked the angel why, with all the delicious food, the people seemed so unhappy. The angel said that there is but one law in the entire kingdom. The man was puzzled.

The angel then took the man to another kingdom on the other side of the universe. There the man found the same banquet table and the same delicious foods. This time the people looked healthy and there was laughter in the air. The man asked the angel, "What is the difference between the two kingdoms?" The angel explained again that there is but one law in the entire kingdom, that, "You must use the eating utensils provided by the management." The problem was that the utensils were ten feet long.

Now, in the first kingdom, where the bodies were frail and there was no laughter, the people were using ten-foot-long forks, knives, and spoons to feed themselves and were literally starving to death. However, in the second kingdom, where there was laughter and the bodies were healthy, the people were using the same ten-foot-long forks, knives, and spoons, but they were reaching across the table and feeding each other.

We cannot shrink from our responsibility to free all of God's children from racial and religious division. If we are going to do what the Lord requires of us then we too must start feeding each other. We must reach across race, class, gender, religion, doctrine, and all superficial barriers, and start feeding each other. No matter how arduous the task or how difficult the moment, we must keep our eyes on the prize and hold on.

THE CHURCH MISSION:
REAL, RELEVANT,
AND REACHABLE

No one can deny that our communities, society, and world are in turmoil. If we look around us, we see that poverty is rampant; race and class conflict is on the rise; disease is widespread; broken families are the rule, not the exception; hopelessness in young people is increasing; and crime and drugs have become the norm in many communities. Without a doubt, all hell has broken out in our midst, and the tragedy is that the church of Jesus Christ has become impotent. Many people who call themselves followers of Christ are standing by watching all of this happen and not doing anything. Somehow, those of us who say we love the Lord have lost our zeal to bring Christ to the forefront of our world.

Dr. T. Garrot Benjamin, pastor of the Light of the World Christian Church, says, "Something is wrong when our children get into crack before they get into the church; get into gangs before they get into God; get into hip-hop before they get into holiness; get into pistols before they get into prayer; get into jail before they get into Jesus;" get into prostitution before they get into praise and worship.

How do we overcome this predicament?

In the Gospel of Matthew 16:18, Jesus says, "Upon this rock, I will build My Church." From all appearances it seems that Jesus has built quite a church. In fact, on nearly every street corner, in every major city, we can find some kind of church. There's a problem, however. Many of the churches, although embellished with the symbols of Jesus, the Christ, have become more like shrines built unto men and women. In other words, we have built churches to serve our own purposes and have not allowed Christ to build His church. A church built by women and men is a church that entertains gossip rather than the gospel of Jesus Christ. A church built by women and men is a church that prides itself on filling seats rather than on saving souls. It hails the choir rather than hailing Christ. It raises hell, rather than raising up disciples. A church built by women and men is a church that teaches a safe gospel rather than a saved gospel. It takes from God rather than gives to God. But oh, how God wants to build His church. God is seeking those who understand that the real church is the church where Christ is the head, the chief cornerstone. The church where Christ is the head is the church that surrenders itself to the authority of Jesus Christ.

As I look around at the state of our world, I believe that God is looking for those who are serious about building the real church of Jesus Christ. In fact, in the first two chapters of the book of Revelation, Jesus gives warning to the church about failing to live out its real purpose. Christ demands that the church get its act together and clean up its mess or else. This means that it's time to do away with all of the self-serving agendas. The only agenda should be Christ's. The purpose of the church is to serve Jesus Christ. In everything that is done on behalf of the church, Christ must be at the center.

For Jesus said, "I, if I be lifted up from the earth, will draw all men unto me." (John 12:32) Essentially, then, when Jesus is lifted, large crowds of people will be attracted to that ministry. I believe we've lost touch with our young people because we are not lifting up Jesus. Our young people have become bored with the church, and some are not even attracted to it in the first place, because they can't see Jesus. And they can't see Jesus because we're in the way. As someone has said, "Some people will never read the Bible, but they will read your life." If we just lift up Jesus, then others will see Jesus through us.

It is not enough, however, for us, the daughters and sons of God, to understand the real purpose of the church. We must also be a relevant church. When Jesus Christ said that "the gates of hell shall not prevail against it," He was, in essence, saying that the church ought to be able to take on the world without the world taking over the church. In other words, a relevant church is powerful enough to influence the climate of the world. We ought to be in the business of turning the world upside down and inside out.

Something is seriously wrong when very few people look to the church for solutions to the many problems and challenges of society. The tragedy is that we, who represent God, have lost so much influence due to our lackadaisical posture that very few people seek us out for solutions to their problems. But why is this? For when the poor needed food, they didn't hesitate to seek out Jesus who fed them with five loaves and two fish. When the sick needed healing, they were brought to Jesus who healed them of all manner of illness and disease. When the lost needed to be found, those who were concerned sought out Jesus and He reminded them that "The Son of man is come to save that which was lost." (Matt. 18:11) When the children needed to be redirected, the children were brought to Him, and He said, "Suffer the little children to come unto me, and forbid them not: for of such is the kingdom of God." (Mark 10:14)

It's time for the church to stand up and be counted and act out of the power that we have been given. No longer can we be tied up and tangled up in our own affairs, while hell is breaking out in our midst. It's time to stop playing church and start being the real church of Jesus Christ that is relevant to the times.

A relevant church is a church where the people of God not only see the problem but are willing to seize the problem. The relevant church is not afraid to take on the problems of the day. I don't care what the political scientist, social strategist, criminologist, psychologist, or economic theorist says about addressing the ills in our society; until the church gets involved, the gates of hell will continue to prevail against us. Yes, only a relevant church can stabilize things.

What characterizes a relevant church?

It is one in which the pastors do more than preach good sermons; they teach out of the Holy Bible. Too many people are suffering in our society, not because it's just the way things are, but because too many Christians are ignorant of God's word. The suffering that we experience is not because of poverty, racism, sexism, and classism. It's not because of drugs, violence, and crime; not because of jealousy, envy, and strife. Our present suffering is because of a lack of knowledge of the word of God. We in the body of Christ need to know that the Holy Bible has an answer to all of the problems we face.

Over the years, though, too many have relied solely on politicians and political parties to save us from the hell we're in. But we must look toward the hills from whence cometh our help, for our help comes from the Lord who made heaven and earth. Yes, it's time for us to be a relevant church, but we can only do it by teaching the word of God.

Many people are talking about how violent our world is becoming and that it is not safe anywhere, and that's the truth. However, we are allowing too much of what the world is saying about the danger to control and dictate our actions. It's a sad day when those of us in the church of God become so paralyzed by fear that we don't take on the problems of society.

In 2 Timothy 1:7, we are reminded that "I have not given you the spirit of fear, but a spirit of power and of love and of a sound mind." And the Twenty-third Psalm reminds us that "Yea, though I walk through the valley of the shadow of death, I will fear no evil for thou art with me; thy rod and thy staff, they comfort me. . . . Surely goodness and mercy shall follow me all the days of my life."

We must become knowledgeable of the Holy Bible and internalize it so that we will be empowered to deal with the evil that is seeking to overcome us. No longer can the focus be on a pie in the sky, by-and-by gospel. We need to know how to deal with the here and now. This characterizes a relevant church.

A relevant church is a church that not only teaches the word of God but also embraces the spiritual essence of life. In the first chapter of Acts, Jesus before he leaves tells his disciples that they would soon receive power. But He was not talking about mental power. He was not talking about financial power. He was not even talking about physical power. He was talking about spiritual power—the Holy Spirit.

If we are going to be a relevant church, then we need to understand the nature of the problems we are seeking to solve. Ephesians 6:12 reminds us that "We wrestle not against flesh and blood, but against principalities, against powers, against rulers of darkness, against spiritual wickedness in high places." In other words, many of the problems we confront are spiritual in nature. Evil is seeking to defeat good, darkness is seeking to put out light, hate is seeking to overpower love, greed is seeking to overcome sacrifice.

We need to understand that spiritual problems have to be fought with spiritual power. Only the Holy Spirit can give us the power we need to ward off the evil and deceptive practices of Satan—and I say deceptive because Satan would have us believe that to feed the hungry is enough. But the Holy Spirit helps us realize that unless we feed their souls, they will continue to be hungry, for "Man shall not live by bread alone, but by every word that proceedeth out of the mouth of God." (Matt. 4:4) A hungry person not only needs to be fed; he needs to be taught how to feed himself. Satan would also have us believe that to clothe the naked is enough. But the Holy Spirit will lead us into the knowledge that unless the person is clothed with the whole armor of God, she or he is still naked. For it is the whole armor of God that enables us to stand against the evil forces. Yes, Satan would have us believe that it is enough just to house the homeless, but the Holy Spirit helps us make sure that their house is built on Jesus, the solid rock, so that they don't go back to being homeless.

We've been having a lot of services and church programs where folks have been shouting and dancing and speaking in tongues, but nothing around them has changed. People say we had a spirit-filled time at church today, and tomorrow it's business as usual. But Jesus said that when the Holy Spirit comes on you, you will receive power. We've been trying to fight all of the problems with our own power, but it's time to let the Holy Spirit in so that it can have a piece of the action.

In the movie *The Empire Strikes Back,* Luke Skywalker was taught by his instructor, Yoda, how to fight against the evil powers and his dark side. One day, the ship landed in the marsh and mud, and Yoda gave Luke Skywalker a demonstration. Yoda looked at the ship with his eyes and the ship floated up and back down. He looked at the ship again and it went up out of the marsh and mud and it came back down. The third time he looked at the ship, the same thing happened. Yoda turned to Luke Skywalker and asked him to do the same as he had done. Luke Skywalker looked at the ship and it didn't move. He looked a second time and the ship still did not move. He looked a third time and with all of the external strength he could muster up, the ship still did not move. Finally, Yoda turned and looked Luke Skywalker in the eye and said, "Son, your problem is that you are trying to use the power, but you've got to allow the power to use you."

63

·

The Holy Spirit cannot be controlled by us; instead, the Holy Spirit controls us. When something controls us, something possesses us, and when something possesses us, it means something has gotten deep inside of us. That's why all throughout the book of Acts, it says that the apostles were filled with the Holy Spirit, not that they had the Holy Spirit. When you're filled with the Holy Spirit, no problem is too difficult to handle, no burden too difficult to bear, no illness to difficult to heal. That's why we can have the Holy Spirit and still not have real power. But when we are filled with the Holy Spirit, we have a power that can take on the world.

I must let you know, however, that it's not enough for a church to be real and relevant if that church isn't reachable. One of the biggest problems with Christians today is that most of us are satisfied with just going to church on Saturday or Sunday morning. Some of us can even be labeled as C.M.E. members, and I don't mean Methodists. I mean that some are Christmas, Mother's Day, and Easter members. The challenge is to move people from mere membership to discipleship.

In Matthew 28:19, Jesus challenges us to "Go and make disciples of all nations." Allow me to clarify what I believe this challenge to be. The word *go* is an action word. It is a powerful word that implies movement. *Go* is the opposite of *stay*, which doesn't require any action.

This is where the concept of church membership breaks down. In general, being a member merely means being on the rolls as a member. Instead of going out of our churches (action), we stay in our churches (inaction). But God is not a stained-glass, four-walled God. God is bigger than any church building will ever be. We serve an omnipresent God, which means He is everywhere at all times. We can't confine Him to our little churches. Jesus says, "Wherever two or three are gathered in My name, there will I be also." (Matthew 18:20) The church, then, is really in each one of us. This is the message Jesus was conveying to Peter when he said, "Upon this rock, I will build my church." Therefore, we should take Jesus wherever we go. You see, people who are outside the body of Christ don't come to the visible church building for various reasons. But if the church is ever going to get inside of them, then we must go and share the church with them.

It's easy for those of us who say we are saved to come to church to hear a good word to satisfy our religious appetite. We cannot just be hearers of the words but must be doers also. It's okay to come to church to sing and dance and shout, but when Jesus comes back, he will not care how high we jumped, but what we did when our feet hit the floor. We can't just stay inside the church. We've got to go out and reclaim our families, our children, and our communities. And we should realize that it's not an option for Christians, it's not a choice but a requirement, because Jesus didn't say, "Will you go?" He didn't say, "Can you go?" He just said, "Go," and go means go!

It's not about membership. It's about discipleship, for a member will only just talk about how good church is but a disciple will model Jesus Christ in his daily life and go out and introduce somebody else to Him.

One of the biggest problems with many Christians is that unlike members of the Nation of Islam, or Jehovah's Witnesses, we only go to the drug house when we want to get high. To the courthouse, when we get charged. To the jailhouse when we, or a family member, gets convicted, and to the schoolhouse when our child is in trouble. We only go to the hospital when we or somebody we know gets sick. To the liquor store when we want a drink, and to the club when we want to hang out. But if those who aren't familiar with Jesus are ever going to know who Jesus really is, then we must go everywhere with His message of hope and salvation. If we stay, the gates of hell will continue to prevail against our children, against our families, against our community, and against our world. We cannot stay; we must go.

The police or military can't do what we can do. Evil cannot be cast out with physical force or a gun. Only in the name of Jesus Christ will the demons of drugs and alcohol addiction, violence and crime, greed, jealousy, envy, and strife be driven out. A reachable church is a church that is filled with people who not only understand, analyze, and talk about the problems, but who go out in the power of God to tackle the problems.

We have the answer. We just need to have enough faith to go out and do something about the problems, knowing that the victory is already ours. If we are going to keep the gates of hell from prevailing against us, then we've got to do more than talk the talk, we've got to walk the walk. "Faith without works is dead."

Jesus Christ is coming back for those who are part of a church without spots or wrinkles. We need to get ourselves in order so that He won't catch us with our work undone. We must work while we have the opportunity because the time will come when we will no longer be able to work. As long as God is with us, there is no need to worry about those who might be against us, for greater is He that is within you than he that is in the world. Therefore, let us resolve to go out, in the name of Jesus, and if there is a problem, go and solve it. If there is a disease, go and cure it. If there is sickness, go and heal it. Where there is hatred, go in love. Where there is violence, go in peace. Where there is sadness, go with joy. Where there is a broken marriage, go work on it and fix it. Where there is a divided family, go and unite it. Where there is an addiction of any kind, go and proclaim deliverance. Where there is injustice, go and stand up for justice. Where there is poverty, go and eliminate it. Where there is hopelessness, go and restore hope. Where there is darkness, go and shed light, for "Ye are the light of the world." (Matt. 5:14)

Let us not wait until the problem knocks at our own door. Let us go to the problem. And we need not worry about the outcome, for Jesus said, "And surely I will be with you always, to the very end of the age." (Matt. 28:20)

CELEBRATE

LIFE

Amerca is a nation of celebration. We love to cele-
brate. We love cakes, balloons, fireworks, cham-
pagne, and noise, plenty of noise. We celebrate New
Year's, Christmas, Hanukkah, Presidents' Day, Valentine's
Day, Labor Day, and Memorial Day. We even celebrate
Columbus Day, even though we know that he did not discover
America, because it is a great excuse to PARTY!!!

It is ironic that if you ask most people, "Why do you celebrate Memorial Day?" or "When is Lincoln's Birthday?" or
"Who was Saint Patrick?" they could not tell you. For many
people, our holidays are nothing more than a nice excuse to
stay at home and do absolutely nothing. It's an excuse to pull
out the grill, turn up the music, and invite over our friends.
We know how to celebrate, but we don't know how to celebrate life.

Look around you: too many babies are dying in their first
year of life; too many children are being abused; too many

mothers with young children are sleeping in our streets; too many teenagers are committing suicide; too many people are dying from AIDS; too many young people are victims of a life of violence and crime. Every fourteen hours a child younger than five years old is murdered; every day 211 American children are arrested for drug abuse; every thirty minutes an American child is arrested for drunk driving ("Children 1990: A Report Card Briefing Book and Action Primer," by the Children's Defense Fund). We need to learn to celebrate life before it's too late. It is life that affords us an opportunity to make a difference in this world. It was Martin Luther King who taught us that all human life is sacred and should be celebrated. That's why he refused to become complacent in the face of social and racial injustices. He understood that these injustices threatened the very essence of life itself. He found refuge in a philosophy that was consistent with his belief in the sanctity of life. It is a philosophy that sought to destroy the life-threatening force while preserving the life itself. The philosophy of nonviolence espoused by Dr. King recognizes that the quality of a person's life is of utmost importance. It is a philosophy that celebrates life.

If we are truly going to celebrate life, we must be honestly committed to working toward eliminating those things in our society that prohibit us from celebrating life, what Dr. King called the triple evils of poverty, racism, and war. Just as he confronted these evils in his day, we too in our time are challenged to confront these evils.

Historically, we have seen that nothing changes in this world unless people unite in direct action. We must remember it was not the goodwill of Presidents Kennedy and Johnson that gave us the Civil Rights Act or the Voting Rights Act. It was the movement in Selma, Birmingham, and Montgomery, in which people were willing to actively participate and sacrifice because they were determined to be free. The people made it happen and that's what made the difference. Now, more than ever before, is the time to take hold of the opportunity to create a society that is more concerned with celebrating life than with destroying life. There is tremendous power when people come together around an issue that is clear, a cause that is just, and a purpose that is righteous.

We must be willing to confront the harsh realities that continue to threaten the quality of life in America and the hope for a bright future. There is talk about life, liberty, and the pursuit of happiness as the basis of the American dream for all citizens. On the other hand, this dream has already become a living nightmare for many, because our nation is indeed a nation divided. Perhaps we have forgotten that we are a nation that was created to be one nation, under God, indivisible, with liberty and justice for all.

Many dreams have been deferred for too long. Many hopes have been dashed against walls. Many aspirations have been bound and gagged. The visions of our youth have been reduced by hopelessness and despair. The cancer of poverty has created a malignancy that has put our entire nation into Intensive Care Economic Arrest. Blood is gushing from the educational artery, the veins of social uplift have collapsed, and the economic and social strategists are running around frantically putting bandages on wounds that have been festering for decades. We are in critical condition and we all need to do what is necessary to stabilize our condition.

We must take a critical look at our individual commitment to human rights. The most fundamental human right is the right to life, but life in this country varies in quality depending on which side of the railroad tracks you were born. For many, the quality of life in America has been snuffed out because of the harsh and inhumane realities of social and economic inequities. Too many in this rich nation of ours are fighting to save their lives from the threat of poverty annihilation. Our brothers and sisters who linger in poverty are being denied life, liberty, and the pursuit of happiness because they are too poor to afford it. If basic human rights are going to be a reality for all, then it's time to put blood back into the lifeline of these victims of our bad social and economic policies.

My challenge to you is to take a critical look at the tainted blood in our social and economic policies that threatens the poor and dispossessed in our nation. Ask yourself, how can this blood be purified so that the masses of those who live in abject poverty can get the blood transfusion they so desperately need to begin enjoying life? Bad policies are the inevitable result of bad policymakers. People are suffering, hurting, and dying in the streets because of some bad public policy decisions that have been made by our elected officials. Children can't read because of bad public policy. Men who want to support families can't get a decent paying job because of bad public policy. Babies are dying because of bad public policy. Drugs are taking over communities because of bad public policy, and the litany goes on. The question is, what are we going to do about it? We must work together daily to ensure that all of our policymakers are accountable to the masses of people, especially to our children who can't vote but whose futures are shaped by public policy. We can no longer allow public officials to enjoy the comfort of the suites if they are going to forget the struggle in the streets. If an elected official has not, does not, and will not support measures that will benefit the disenfranchised, then that official should be the target of public outcry. This means it's time to take it to the streets.

Furthermore, we must hold accountable public officials who make policy according to dollar bills waved in front of their eyes. Our society cannot afford to allow our public officials to behave this way. It indicates that they have no respect for human life. We cannot afford to sit by idly while our government and the people in power play these kinds of games with our lives and the lives of our children; we cannot sit by idly while backs are turned to the poor and doors are closed on the dispossessed as money is passed underneath the table. If there is ever going to be a revival of hope in our nation, it will be because we, the people, decided to rise up, speak up, stand up, and never shut up until social and economic justice is secured for *all* God's children.

It's time to stop sitting around the table with the enemy of human rights; drinking from the cup of deception; feasting on the main course of uncalculated military maneuvers; picking at the tossed salad of double standard politics; eating the dessert of governmental corruption and societal decay. Time is running out and we must fight the fight for true freedom and justice.

If we can't get rid of bad policymakers through our democratic election process, then the alternative is to counteract what they do. This means we have to internalize what my father said: "When evil men plot, good men must plan; when evil men burn and bomb, good men must commit themselves to the glories of love. When evil men would seek to perpetuate an unjust status quo, good men must bring into being a real order of justice." These must become more than mere words, but must become the blueprint for restoring optimism in the American dream.

What are these social and economic policies that threaten the quality of life in this country? In the first place, we have to understand that every hour during the current fiscal year, our federal government spends approximately $33.7 million on national defense; $23.6 million on the national debt; $8.7 million on the S&L bailout; $2.1 million on education, and $1.8 million on children's health care. This translates into fifty cents out of every tax dollar for the military industrial complex but only two cents for education and one cent for children's health care. Clearly, we place a higher premium on programs of death and destruction than we do on programs that enhance human life. Ours has become more a thing-oriented society than a people-oriented society. No wonder we find it difficult to celebrate life in this country. But it's time to seek an America that is truly of, for, and by the people—where profits are not more important than people.

Probably the greatest hindrance to ridding our society of violence is how little we value life. Something is wrong when our young people can take a life to possess a material object, or for no reason, and feel no remorse for it. Something is wrong when law enforcement officers can beat a man senseless and get away with it. This means that we have done a poor job of promoting the sanctity of life in this nation.

Think about this: since the founding of our nation, violence has been an acceptable way of life. Whether we talk about the American Revolution, the Civil War, World War I, World War II, lynch mobs, the Vietnam War, the war in the Persian Gulf, or the death penalty, violence has been the American way. The irony and tragedy is that these wars began as peace efforts but have only led to further chaos and confusion and more violence. America has a reputation of being the most violent nation in the world. We glory in financing sophisticated systems of weaponry in the way that some other countries glory in financing their systems of education and technology. This means that we place more value on the destruction rather than the preservation of life. But the Bible reminds us that you reap what you sow. We have sown seeds of violence all over the world, and we are now victims of the very violence we perpetuate. Our people have watched the way we have conducted ourselves in the world community and many have concluded that violence is an acceptable means for resolving conflict and differences. I surmise this is why America far exceeds other industrialized countries in the number of handgun murders. Many murders are an outgrowth of the drug culture and gangs. In many ways, gang violence is no more than a replica of the many conflicts that this nation has had with other nations. It's about territory and protecting interests.

Violence in our society, however, is not just tied to the examples we've set in our international dealings. Most of the violence we witness is the natural outgrowth of bad social and economic policies. Is a man or woman who steals a loaf of bread because he or she is hungry a criminal or a victim? Is a teenager who sells drugs to support his family and put food on the table for his younger brothers and sisters a criminal or a victim? I suggest that they are both criminals and victims. In many ways their acts can be traced to those social and economic conditions that create an atmosphere that might lead one to make such decisions. These unfortunate realities are born of poverty in the midst of great affluence. As long as we ignore the needs of those in poverty-stricken America, we will continue to see more violence and crime.

Violence is so much a part of the social fabric in our society that even the entertainment industry has sought to justify it under the First Amendment right to free speech. But rights without responsibility leave everybody vulnerable. Every day we are bombarded with violence. The average American is exposed to six to eight acts of violence on television per hour during prime time. And Saturday children's programming exposes our children to between twenty and twenty-five acts of violence per hour.

We have accepted violence so much that it is like a shadow that will not go away. You turn on the television to watch the news—violence. You pick up the morning paper to see what is going on in the world—violence. You go to class and a classmate will not speak, or you go to work and a co-worker won't speak—violence. The professor, or your supervisor, got up on the wrong side of the bed—violence. Everywhere we turn there is violence.

The question then becomes, where is the peace? Where are the teachings that would provide us an alternative to the madness that is all around? The entire world order, it appears, is based on a model of competition rather than a model of cooperation. The model many have been taught is rugged individualism rather than compassionate communalism. This is, perhaps, the reason behind the violent attack on the skater Nancy Kerrigan. When one's values and principles are dictated by a model of competition, they inevitably lead down a dark corridor of uncertainty and a sure path to violent interaction.

Too many have gotten caught up in this cycle of violence, this step-on-everybody mentality, and in the process have lost respect for human life. My father fought with all he had to break this pattern of rugged individualism. Dare we go on as if nothing is happening? Dare we close our eyes and refuse to see the devastation all around us?

It is time for concerned people, especially concerned young people, to rise up in righteous indignation and say, "Enough is enough." Somebody must say that we are tired of violence. We are tired of murders. We are tired of children being abused and neglected. We are tired of gang wars. We are tired of young people dying in our streets.

If we are serious about peace, then we are in dire need of something new and something different. We've tried violence for a long time, and what we have gotten is just more violence. Violence only begets violence. As my father said in his 1964 Nobel Peace Prize acceptance speech:

In spite of temporary victories, violence never brings permanent peace. It solves no social problem. It merely creates new and more complicated ones. Violence is immoral because it thrives on hatred rather than love. Violence is impractical because it is a de-

scending spiral ending in destruction for all. It is immoral because it seeks to humiliate the opponent
rather than win his understanding. It destroys community and makes brotherhood impossible. It leaves society in monologue rather than dialogue. Violence ends
up defeating itself.

It's past the time to cut off this chain of violence in our society. We need people who, like my father, will confront the
very heart of the beast of violence. One of the ways to fight
this beast and begin celebrating life is to put our energies into
encouraging our elected officials to regulate "the violence industry," which includes toy companies, the entertainment industry (especially film and cartoon makers), video arcade
operators, and gun manufacturers and sellers. Regulations
without enforcement are useless; therefore, we can no longer
allow this industry to inculcate and promote violence at the
expense of losing more lives to gun violence. If we can vigor-
ously regulate the sale of medicine and limit the advertise-
ment of cigarettes because of their effect on human health,
certainly we can and must regulate those industries that contribute to the number one cause of death (murder) for many
of our young people. It's a life and death issue and should be
considered a health care problem.

Finally, to celebrate life, we must build bridges of understanding. We must build relationships with all people regardless of their station in life.

One of the greatest tragedies in this nation is that people
of color, especially African Americans, have seldom been recognized for their gifts, talents, and intelligence. It is still a fact

that if you are black in America, you are the last hired and the first fired. It is a common practice among the majority race to consider an articulate and intelligent African American exceptional. Segregated neighborhoods and schools are still the rule and not the exception.

Taking on the giant of racism is no easy proposition, but it must be done. We must learn to live together as brothers and sisters because our destinies are tied together. All life is interrelated and, as my father so often said, "what affects one directly affects all indirectly." This means that I cannot be all that I ought to be until you are all that you ought to be, and you cannot be all that you ought to be until I am all that I ought to be. It's time to acknowledge that everybody has something significant that they can bring to the table. And although it is risky to talk about building relationships with people who for a long time have had fears, doubts, or inhibitions about us, we must take these risks for the sake of a more harmonious society.

Now is the time for men and women of moral courage and ethical convictions to stand up and be counted. No more hiding behind our titles and positions—it's time to embody a commitment to serve this present age, keeping in mind that every person is a human being to be valued.

To look is one thing, to see what you look at is another. To understand what you see is a third. To learn from what you understand is still something else. But to act on what you learn is what really counts. Today, all of us must ask ourselves, what am I acting on? How far am I willing to go?

Surely by now you are saying, "But I am only one person; how can I possibly enhance the quality of life in America?" Remember, every worthwhile invention began with one person.

Every progressive mechanism for social uplift, every major movement that changed the course of history began with one person. So while you are just one person and you cannot do everything, you can do something. What you can do you ought to do, and what you ought to do, by God's grace, you must do. We must make things happen in our own organizations, our own communities, our own institutions, and our own political circles.

Yes, it's time to celebrate life, to make sure that we get the guns off our streets and stop killing each other. To celebrate life is to protect our young people from heavy exposure to violence from the television screen to the silver screen, from the toy companies to video arcade operators. To celebrate life is to work until every American has health care and none need die because of a lack of funds. To celebrate life is to ensure that everyone who wants a job can find a job, and to work to create a society that makes the needs of its children and its elderly a top priority. To celebrate life means that we will not rest until those in the African American community who can hit the ball and shoot the hoop can also own the team that hits the ball and shoots the hoop. To celebrate life means that we will not rest until America is America for all its citizens, black and white, Native American, Asian American, Hispanic, Jew and Gentile, rich and poor, educated and uneducated.

The bird celebrates life by saying tweet-tweet, the cat by saying meow-meow, the dog by saying bow-wow, the cow by saying moo-moo. We celebrate life by building bridges of understanding, tearing down walls of indifference, establishing a haven for justice, erecting a monument to peace, securing a foundation of hope, and serving a God who is *able*.

PART TWO

COMFORTING

THE

DISTURBED

HEALING
THE BROKEN LIFE

A s I have reflected upon my role as a minister, I've come to the realization that there is a commonality between what I do and what those in the health care profession do—especially nurses. Both are helping and healing professions, taking broken lives and seeking to put them back together. In essence, we help to mend lives. And what I have learned is that even in our own brokenness, we can be healers. Dr. Henry Nouwen, in his book *The Wounded Healer,* talks about how we have the capacity in our brokenness to heal, help, and encourage others. In fact, he says that we are called to look after our own wounds while simultaneously being prepared to heal the wounds of others. The good news is that we don't have to be perfect to be healers. An old legend in the Talmud sheds light on this point.

Rabbi Yoshua ben Levi came upon Elijah the prophet while he was standing at the entrance of Rabbi Simeron ben Yohai's cave. He asked Elijah, "When will the Messiah come?"

Elijah replied, "Go and ask him yourself."

"Where is he?"

"Sitting at the gates of the city."

"How shall I know him?"

"He is sitting among the poor, covered with wounds. The others unbind all their wounds at the same time and then bind them up again. But he unbinds one at a time and binds it up again, saying to himself, 'Perhaps I shall be needed. If so, I must always be ready so as not to delay for a moment.' "

Like the Messiah in this story, we are called upon to be ready and willing to offer ourselves, with our own wounds, as a source for healing power. Perhaps the best way we can do this is to develop a relationship between our head, our heart, and our hands. Some helpers are good at the head level—they have cognitive ability and knowledge—while some are good with matters of the heart—the emotions and compassion. But their heads and hearts never communicate with each other. Some helpers do a lot—the Bible talks about people who have zeal, but not according to knowledge. Then there are those of us who do but perhaps not from the heart, so motives need to be questioned.

As we reflect upon building partnerships and relationships, and as we seek to understand the interdependency of our helping professions, we should focus on the importance of the head, the heart, and the hands to what we do. Through this we will be able to create a synergy, or a coming together, that will enable us to be more effective as we care for those who are hurting.

First, let us focus on the head, which encompasses the knowledge, the self-image, and the attitudes that we bring to our caring for others. Without a doubt, how I feel about my-self is going to affect how I feel about the person I'm caring for. If I have a low self-image, certain things I do will reflect this fact to the person and may inhibit their healing. Often we find ourselves in situations where we are snapping and saying things that are merely a projection of the way we feel about ourselves, rather than an accurate assessment of the worth of the person we're seeking to help. But if I have a positive sense of self-worth, I will treat the person accordingly. The words, the language, and the behavior that I exemplify will convey to the person the sense that "I'm okay, you're okay." This is par-ticularly important in the area of rehabilitation, because often the person's self-esteem has been challenged by the circum-stances that brought that person to you.

Furthermore, although we are professionals, we are hu-man beings with opinions, and we often bring certain atti-tudes to our relationships with those we seek to help. It behooves us to examine these attitudes and make sure that they are not hindering the support we are giving. Of course, a positive attitude is of utmost importance when we are with those who bring their brokenness to us, because their distress can often leave them feeling defeated. If our minds and our thoughts are always on unrewarding and negative things, it is conceivable that we will convey negative messages to and cre-ate negative environments for those we are seeking to bring back to wholeness.

Therefore, if we are going to come from a place of em-powerment in the helping profession, and if we are going to build these relationships and partnerships, it is incumbent upon us to have a positive frame of reference. If our story is always one of gloom and doom, then nobody is going to want to work or even to be around us. Our conversations always ought to be positive, for a negative thought leads to negative talk which leads to a negative walk, so our task is to work on getting our heads in order. As an anonymous writer has said:

> If you think you are beaten, you are.
> If you think you dare not, you don't.
> If you think you are out-classed, you are.
> If you'd like to win, but you think you can't, it's almost certain you won't.
> If you think you'll lose, you've lost.
> For out in the world you'll find that success begins with a person's will; it's all in the state of mind.

Because we are dealing with people who bring to us their hurts and their pains, we should shape our attitudes and self-awareness so that we can relate effectively to them in their pain.

Furthermore, we need to examine our hearts—the center of our emotions, feelings, and compassion. It is from the heart that our passions emerge. It is out of the heart that our love, our fears, our anger come forth. It is incumbent upon us to examine our hearts and make sure we are not one of those who doesn't have the heart to be there, who genuinely doesn't care. For this type of person, helping is merely a job. If we are to be effective helpers, helping cannot be a vocation but must be an avocation—a calling, a commitment, a passion to help, to assist, and to be with people in their brokenness. It takes a special kind of person who has this kind of heart.

In talking about the heart, I remember what my father so often said: Anybody can be great, because anybody can serve. All you need is a heart full of grace and a soul generated by love. I have come to realize that what is most needed in the helping profession is a sincere love, a love not defined by what it gets in return or how it can benefit but a love that is willing to take whatever risks are necessary to nurse "the other" back to wholeness and healing.

As a society, we have failed to achieve genuine compassion. We tend to have sympathy rather than empathy for someone. We feel more comfortable feeling sorry for rather than sorry with someone. I suggest that oftentimes it is our fears that hold us back, because we are afraid that if we invest too much of ourselves in somebody else's world we might lose something in the process. For those of us who are called to care for others, it is not unusual for us to lay down some part of our lives as a part of the helping process. Courage requires that we venture into the unknown with the other, to experience that which we have not experienced. Of course, we don't know what will happen to the other person, what he or she will become, or even what changes will occur within ourselves. But we must be willing to risk that which is dearest to us in order to create a healing atmosphere.

Jesus Christ risked his very life to meet the needs of people. The Holy Bible says that He was moved with compassion as He looked upon the illnesses, as He looked upon the multitude. And yes, I'm sure He was busy. He was, perhaps, on His way to a seminar, to a medical society conference, or to a staff meeting with His disciples, but He was moved with compassion. He could not help himself. There was something inside of Him. And the question is, do we have this something inside of us? That something we cannot get from school or from training or supervision; but something from within, from our spirit; that feeling of wanting to serve; that feeling of wanting to help others. There are so many who look down on people, but we should never look down on people except to lift them up. This is what it means to have our heart in the right place.

Other considerations of the heart that I believe we as caregivers are called upon to embrace are referred to in the book *On Caring* by Milton Mayeroff: they are patience and trust. Patience means sticking with people as they grow at their own pace and not becoming overwhelmed. It also means that when those we are helping get stuck at a particular stage in the healing process that we not give up but that we move to what I call the ministry of being as opposed to doing: by speaking or listening, sitting with the other and sharing in the silence, or actually physically withdrawing for the sake of our own sanity and enabling them to come to grips with their thoughts and feelings at that moment.

At this point trust is very important—trust in the process, in the relationship, and in other people's potential to be healed. This means not overdoing it—pushing people beyond their limits—and also not overprotecting—doing for them what they can do for themselves. This is particularly critical because we don't want the supportive relationship that we have established to be used as a crutch by the other. This only inhibits growth by continuing dependency. In his book, *The Seven Habits of Highly Effective People,* Stephen Covey says that people move on a maturity continuum from dependence to independence to interdependence. He says that "dependent people need others to get what they want. Independent people can get what they want through their own efforts. Interdependent people combine their own efforts with the efforts of others to achieve their greatest success." It is important that we get in touch with our own level of maturation because it is not unusual for a dependent person to create a relationship that is dependent. In other words, if we have a great need for a dependent relationship, it is unlikely that we will be able to help another move to the level of independence, and certainly not to interdependence. As Covey says, "Interdependence is a choice only independent people can make." If we find that we are creating a dependent relationship, it is important to draw the line and say no to those things that the people we're caring for can or should be doing for themselves, or delegate the work to others who work with us. These are the matters of the heart that are important for those of us in the helping profession.

Finally, I must say that there are people who have the knowledge—who have their head in order—and who have their heart in order, but they never put what they know and what they feel into practice. This is where the rubber hits the road, for as the Bible says, "Faith without works is dead." The hands are our working tools, our action. It is the doing part of our professions—the application. Look at the hands. Some of us have nice, soft, smooth hands. But sometimes, the hands have to get dirty. Sometimes the hands have to get scarred. Sometimes it's important to have a few calluses on our hands.

There is a story told of a lady whose daughter always complained about her mother's hands. Her hands were so ugly and the daughter was so embarrassed about it and could never understand why Mom would even display these hands in public. The daughter even got to the point where she was getting ready to receive her degree from college and asked her mother not to come to the graduation ceremony because she was embarrassed by those hands. She didn't want anyone to see how grotesque, how distorted those hands were. As a result, her mother didn't come to her graduation, but other members of the family did. They asked, "Where is your mom?" The daughter replied, "I asked Mom not to come because I am embarrassed by her hands and I know people would be looking at her." They said, "You should talk to your mom about her hands." Well, after she got her degree, she went back and talked to her mother. She said, "Mom, you never told me why your hands look so bad." The mother said, "I never told you because you never asked." She went on to say, "One day, you were playing in the kitchen with fire and your dress caught on fire. I didn't have time to get water or a towel. With my bare hands, I snuffed out that fire so that you would not be burned. And look at how beautiful your skin is as a result. These are the hands that saved you from burning."

What's in your hands? Look at them. Do they bear any scars? Do they bear any mark of wiping away tears? Mending any broken hearts? Alleviating any pains? It is time for us to get the head, the heart, and the hand together.

We are called upon to get involved and make things happen in the lives of those we care for. This is when our hands are working. As helpers, we are called upon to help people live out their potential. We are called upon to help people achieve an attitude of acceptance toward the unchangeable aspects of their lives; to learn to live with the "givens" of their situation; to not let the givens keep them from doing whatever they are capable of doing toward achieving wholeness and healing. By doing this we don't keep people disabled or handicapped or helpless for the sake of keeping our own jobs. That's why, as we engage our hands and start doing something, we must remember that there is a temptation to keep the helpless and disabled in their condition so that we have a profession. One's calling, one's mission, though, is to help them become whole, even if it goes against our grain. We are to set the captives free. We must not get so caught up in paperwork and meeting performance standards that we lose sight of our primary mission, which is to heal the wounded. We must always work for the healing of others.

In the book of Nehemiah in the Bible, the people had a mind to work. They were faced with brokenness because the wall that surrounded Jerusalem had been torn down. In an effort to rebuild the wall, everyone had to rebuild around their house for the purpose of self-preservation and self-interest. The interesting point, though, is that it wasn't for self-interest or self-preservation's sake because in the end the whole wall was built and the whole nation of Israel was protected. In doing their part, they were part of a team. Where there were empty spots, they filled them in. They filled in the breaches and the gaps.

As we seek to rebuild the lives of people who have experienced brokenness, no one should fall through the gaps or go unnoticed. If we each do our part by coordinating our head, heart, and hand, then we will be part of a team, a partnership, that helps to nurse people back to wholeness.

A CALL
TO CHRISTIAN
MANHOOD

If we were to take an honest look at our families, our relationships, our communities, and our nation, we would have to conclude that there is a missing link. Consider the irony: we have an abundance of wealth, and yet poverty is still an overwhelming reality. We have a host of antiviolence programs, and yet homicide is the leading cause of death among black males between fifteen and thirty-four years of age and is the second leading cause of death among females within the same age group. We have several conflict-resolution programs, yet people are still packing guns and using them when someone pushes them to the limit. We've pumped a lot of money into this war on drugs, and yet drugs continue to flow into the inner cities. We have many marriage enrichment seminars and books, yet divorce is the rule and not the exception.

If you ask me, it appears that we are a nation divided against itself. In Mark 3:24, Jesus said, "If a kingdom (nation) be divided against itself, that kingdom cannot stand." We've mustered up all of the money and manpower to address these ironies, but to little avail. Something indeed is missing. We've done study on top of study and started program after program, but out of all the studies that have been done on urban America and the programs that have been implemented to address the problems, few if any of them have interfaced with the religious community. In other words, God is left out of the solution. Why?

One of the primary reasons is the lack of godly men who are willing to stand out and stand up, speak out and speak up. Why do black boys find comfort in gangs, drugs, violence, materialism? It's because there are too few visible black Christian men. It's a sad day when the only men our black boys see are drug dealers, rap artists, and basketball players. What's missing? Black Christian men who are willing to stand out as examples of what it means to be a real man in a misdirected society. Our Christian men ought to leave the church house ready to take on the crack house. Our Christian men ought to leave some woman's bedroom and find some boy's classroom. It's time for Christian men to stand out and show the way. The only things that our boys and our girls know how to glorify are sex, materialism, and violence. The message that they see all around them is mo' money, mo' sex, mo' violence. Our young people, especially our boys, need to see mo' Jesus.

There is a familiar phrase in the African American community that we use when we feel that somebody has forsaken their commitment to the race—we say that they have sold out. Well, I thought about the concept of being sold out and concluded that there's nothing wrong with being sold out—but it's who you're sold out to. In Luke 14:26, Jesus told the crowds that were following Him that "if anyone comes to Me and does not hate his father and mother, his wife and his children, his brothers and his sisters, even his own life, he cannot be My disciple." Jesus was saying, in essence, you've got to be sold out to Him. But you know, some folks can be sold out to Jesus, and the right person or the right thing can come along and buy them out. That's why we need Christian men and women who are not only sold out to Jesus but who have let Jesus buy them out.

Are you sold out and bought out by Jesus today? Our young people need to see leaders who put Christ first, not money, not jobs, not sex, not crack cocaine. They've been deceived too long now. They need to know that Jesus, not money, not sex, not crack cocaine, not gang-banging, but Jesus is the way, the truth, and the life. But they will only know it when Christian men start leading by example. I challenge every Christian man to set an example of what it means to be sold out to and bought out by Christ. If we are going to see our inner cities change and our young people living more constructive lives, then Christian men ought to stand out in our families, communities, and society. As Dr. Anthony T. Evans, founder of The Urban Alternative in Dallas, Texas, writes, the main problem in our society is not that we don't have enough money or enough programs, nor that we can't solve our problems. The problem is that we don't have enough disciples, men and women who understand that their purpose in life is to represent Christ (*America's Only Hope,* Chicago: Moody Press, 1990). And since Christ's own words suggest that to follow Him is to sell out to Him, then we need more African American men who are sold out to and bought out by Jesus. I suggest that a sold out and bought out man of God is a man who is a saved, sanctified servant of Christ. Our communities and our society desperately need men who are saved, sanctified servants of Christ.

If we look around, we can conclude that those of us who call ourselves Christians have forgotten or misunderstood our purpose. Many of us attend church once a week so that we can feed our own souls to make it through the week. But that's Churchianity, not Christianity. Some of us may even be involved in various ministries of the Church, but strangely enough we see very little impact on the community. We have more revivals, and yet nothing changes. We need to better understand what it means to be a saved, sanctified servant of Christ.

A saved man of God is one who knows more than Jesus' name, for even a computer knows Jesus' name if programmed so. When Romans 10:9 says, "If thou shalt confess with thine mouth that Jesus is Lord, and believe in thine heart that God raised Him from the dead," it's talking about a relationship. Any time a person gets into your heart, that person has to be special to you. The only way a person becomes special is through a relationship. Too many men of God only know Jesus by name and are afraid to have a relationship with Jesus. For you see, to have a special relationship is to get intimate, and for a lot of men that's a scary proposition because it means commitment, it means sacrifice—giving up something to get something. It means becoming vulnerable. Because of the macho image that society encourages, many men have a problem being vulnerable. And when one speaks of vulnerability in a relationship, it means that the person is putting his trust in another person or surrendering himself to another person's will. This means that a person gives up the desire to be in control. It's time for us to stop trying to control everything and solve every problem. If we serve an omnipotent—all powerful and omniscient—all knowing God, then shouldn't we surrender ourselves to Him?

The leaders of the world have tried to solve our problems with world solutions, but we've only gotten more confusion and more corruption. We need to hear from God, and the only way we can is if we have more men who are willing to say, Not my will, but God's will be done. Christ wants saved men who aren't afraid to get vulnerable with Him. That's why He said, "If any man will come after Me, let him deny himself, and take up his cross, and follow Me." (Matt. 16:24) A saved man of God then is a surrendered vessel.

A second point about being in a relationship with another person is that over time you identify with that person. Identification breeds assimilation. In other words, you become like the person. When two people are in a relationship for a long time, we often say that they begin to look like each other. What happens is that the more time you spend with a person, the more you begin to pick up characteristics of that person. The old you merges into the other person. I guess this is why the Bible says that two shall become one, because the two begin to act alike, talk alike, think alike, and look alike.

The reason that we don't see any evidence of God in our society is that there are not enough people modeling Christ in their lives. Men who claim to be in Christ are acting and thinking just like the men who are not in Christ. Our boys ought to be able to tell the difference between a man sold out to Christ and one who is not. We need men to show them what it means to love each other, not kill each other. There used to be a time when our young people saw examples of men who lived out of their Judeo-Christian values. Our boys saw men who respected a woman who held on to her virginity until marriage. Our boys saw men who practiced fidelity in marriage. Our boys saw men who knew they were men and challenged any man who didn't act male. Now, it seems our boys only see men who scorn virgins and celebrate promiscuity, who pre-plan divorces through prenuptial agreements, and men who accept homosexuality as an alternative lifestyle. Something is missing.

We need men who understand that it's all right to be like the one you love. In fact, when a person first gets saved it's like falling in love. When a person falls in love, he wants to be near the one he loves. He wants to live for the other person. Therefore, falling in love with Christ should lead one to wanting to live for Christ. This is what it means to be sanctified. "Sanctified" is not a religion. We've gotten it all mixed up. To be sanctified is to be set apart for God's purposes. Our lifestyles are supposed to reflect Christ.

But where are all the sanctified folks? Sanctified men shake up things, and the reason I know that is because any time Christ came on the scene, leaders trembled with fear. They knew that Christ didn't tolerate government corruption, economic exploitation, and social degradation. A sanctified man says enough is enough. He won't tolerate drug dealers preying on our young boys. He won't tolerate our boys disrespecting our girls or anybody else for that matter. He won't tolerate the negative images of our people, especially our men.

A sanctified man cannot be intimidated by the consequences of living for Christ. My father used to say, "A man is not fit to live unless he has found something worth dying for." However, many of our boys have gotten mixed up. They feel that a real man ought to be willing to die for something he believes in; the problem is they are dying for the wrong reasons. They are dying for death and a feeling, for materialism and greed. But Jesus said, "Whosoever will lose his life for My sake shall find it." (Matt. 16:25)

There used to be a time in the African American community when men would put their lives on the line for freedom and justice; but today, too many men are sitting back in their seats of comfort, afraid to leave their safety zones. As a result, our families and our communities are falling apart. We need sanctified men who know that being sanctified is more than looking holy or talking holy; being sanctified is living holy. Living holy means being willing to stand up and willing to die for truth. Our boys and girls need to see more men who are willing to die for truth, not tennis shoes, not Starter jackets, not fancy cars, not crack cocaine. Things have gotten out of hand. There was a time when *crack* was just a crack in the wall, *coke* was just soda pop, and *grass* was just something that you cut in your front yard.

We're spending too much time on the wrong things. Too much has slipped by us, and now our children are dying to make a living because we are not making a life for our children—I say our children, because whether or not they're our biological children they are still ours. As the old African proverb says, "It takes an entire village to raise a child."

Every man who knows Jesus, whether he has children or not, ought to be introducing as many boys as possible to Jesus. We can do all the talking and training and mentoring we want to do, but if we don't let them meet Jesus for themselves, they are more apt to go back to their old ways.

Our boys need something on the inside to sustain them when we're not around. Why is it that a drug dealer can introduce a young boy to the drug trade and put him in charge of sales, while he goes off to do something else, and when he comes back that boy will have carried out his responsibilities? It's fear. If drug dealers can put fear of themselves inside our young boys, why is it that we can't put the fear of God inside our boys? Fear of God only comes when one is "born again." One who is born again not only depends on God but also obeys God's commands and precepts. This means that God has gotten deep down inside the heart, and when God gets deep down inside the heart, not only do you start to think like God, but you start behaving like God would behave if He were in the situation. This is what I mean by sanctification.

Look at your family, look at your community, look at your marriage. What would God do? We ask the political scientist, the social analyst, and the economic theorist what we should do about the crisis in our nation, and in many cases we've followed their advice, but we've made very little progress. It's time for those of us who say that we're in Christ to do what Christ would do if He were in the situation, and the only way that we will know what Christ would do is if we study the

99

word of God. The Bible says that "My people are destroyed for lack of knowledge [of the Word of God]." (Hos. 4:6)

Finally, God wants Christian men to stand out in the area of servanthood. The Bible says, "Whoever would be great among you must be your servant." (Matt. 20:26) In other words, a servant gets "self" out of primary focus, including self's ego. One of the biggest problems in the African American community is that we have too many chiefs and not enough Indians. Everybody wants to call the shots, to be in charge, to get the credit and be seen. Nobody wants to do what is required to heal our community.

The reason, I think, that my father is now revered by many is that he was less concerned with being out front and more concerned with doing God's will. When a person is serving Christ first, he doesn't have to worry about being out front because God will elevate him. God is looking for men who will forget about doing things for their own praise and glory, and will do things to praise and glorify God.

How does one know when one is truly serving God? Check your motives. There are 24 hours in a day and 168 hours in a week. How much of that time do you devote to the kingdom of God? Who made it possible for you to have that job? Does anybody on that job know that you are saved and sanctified, or do they just treat you as one of the boys? Even on our jobs we are to glorify God. When was the last time you made a substantial difference in someone's life? If you can't remember, then I suggest that you are serving self and not serving Christ. How many men can honestly say that they introduced somebody to Christ?

Of the salary that you bring home, how much of it do you

give back to God? Think about this——most of us go to a nice restaurant, and if the service is good we leave a 15 percent tip for someone who is a total stranger just because he gave us good service. How is it that we can be blessed by God every day and yet rarely give him the 10 percent that He asks for? Don't you know that if more of us gave our 10 percent we could address every problem we face in the African American community? We shouldn't have to beg, borrow, and steal. There's enough money to go around if we just use it the right way.

Maybe the problem is that our hearts are not in the right place. Instead of serving God, we serve man and the world. The Bible reminds us, "Wherever your treasure is there will your heart be also."

If we are going to take back our streets and our children in the African American community, then it's time for men of God who are sold out to Christ and saved, sanctified servants to stand out and take charge. No more running and hiding; it's time to be bold for the Lord. Real men of Christ aren't afraid to take over the crack house, the state house, the White House, and even the courthouse. God is ready to do a new thing, if you will but surrender your old self to Him.

There's a story about two men who worried the king by arguing over whether or not a man had to be born a gentleman or if he could, through habit and discipline and education, become a gentleman. So the king sent them out on their merry way and said, "I'm going to settle this argument once and for all. I want both of you to take one year and go all over the world and find evidence for your position. And in one year I want you back in my court to give me evidence supporting your position."

The first man, who had said that one can become a gentleman through habit, discipline, and education, took off and stayed away for almost an entire year. One day, tired and frustrated, he sat down in his seat in a restaurant and he saw a cat. This was no ordinary cat. It had been trained to stand on its hind legs and to carry a small tray in its two front paws. To the man's amazement, this cat was bringing him his order—a glass of wine. Immediately, he realized that through habit, training, and discipline, this cat was able to do unnatural things. He paid a fortune for the cat and reported back to the king.

Word got out about this amazing cat and what it was doing, and it drove the other man, who was in the competition with him, to the wall of despair. He, too, had gone all over the world, but had returned empty-handed. However, two days before they were actually due back in the king's court, the second man, who had said one had to be born a gentleman, passed by a little shop and saw something that brought a smile to his face. He went in and purchased it, but kept quiet until he got into the king's court.

The king called the first man. He bowed to the king and turned loose his cat. The cat, dressed in a royal suit and tie, stood up on his hind legs and got the tray with a glass of wine. As he walked down the red royal carpet, the whole court erupted in applause and looked with sympathy at the second man.

Finally, the second man bowed to the king and set down a box and opened it. Out walked five white mice. The cat forgot his training, forgot his education, and lost his discipline.

He dropped the tray of wine, reverted back to his old nature, and ran after the mice.

After two or three hours, the cat came back with his royal suit all twisted and torn. He was bruised and battered from the chase. The king said, "It is settled once and for all—one must be born a gentleman."

It makes no difference how much education, money, prestige, power, or sex you acquire; if the time, court, invitation, and place are right, you will go back to your old nature. That's why you have to be born again, because only when you are born again do you have the new nature of God planted in your heart. We have a lot of people who are saved in their head and not in their heart. There are only eighteen inches between the head and the heart and some of us are going to miss heaven by eighteen inches.

So if you are having problems truly serving God, then just say, "Give me a clean heart so I may serve thee. Lord, fix my heart so that I may be used by thee, for I am not worthy of all these blessings. Give me a clean heart, and I'll follow thee."

Yes, "Blessed are the pure in heart, for they shall see God." (Matt. 5:8) What's your heart's desire? Are you a saved, sanctified servant of Christ? If so, let your light so shine before men that they may see your good works and glorify not you or your money, cars, prestige, or fame, but glorify your Father who is in heaven.

WHEN GOD
CREATED
WOMEN

An old Chinese proverb says, "God could not be everywhere, so He gave us mothers." Women and mothers have greatly inspired our society since its inception: women who have dared to speak up in the face of grave injustice, or who even in their silence say more than presidents and kings. Women's touch has calmed the raging madness of conquerors and warriors.

I don't know of any great leader who got here other than through a woman. No matter where we go in life, we must first come through a mother. Think about it—every man and woman on the face of this earth has been birthed, bathed, burped, bounced, boosted, and bosomed by a woman. Over 50 percent of the world's population is female, and women have unquestionably been the primary nurturers.

For decades, we as women were locked out of mainstream American life. Many were deceived into believing that we women were unaware of what was going on. Now, all around the world, women are starting to exercise their God-given talents. Margaret Thatcher, Corizon Aquino, Coretta Scott King, Myrlie Evers, Hillary Rodham Clinton, Janet Reno, and Marian Wright Edelman are just the beginning of a huge wave that is quickly approaching every town, city, state, and country.

I am convinced that if God had intended for women to be trampled upon, He would have taken a bone from the foot of man to make her. If He had intended her to always follow after man, He would have used a back bone, and if He had intended for her to be kicked around, He would have used a knee bone. But God intended for women to be companions of men, and so He made her of a rib bone, from the side of man, so that she would hold his hand along life's journey.

So much has happened to women in the last fifty years. Fads have come and gone, from miniskirts to long dresses, back to miniskirts, and yet there is a legacy of courage and tenacity among women. We have witnessed it in women's achievements in government, finance, entrepreneurship, commerce, education, international diplomacy, athletics, politics, business, and ministry. In spite of the obstacles women have had to overcome, the mountains we have had to climb, the abuse we have endured, the slander we have had to rise above, "We've come a long way, baby, to get where we are today."

And how did we make it? How did we get here? We put our trust and faith not in man, but in God. God has brought us this far. Even so, I can hear us saying, "Please be patient, because God is not through with me yet."

Our history is a history of struggle, and struggle at times means taking a stand. We have always stood for that which is decent, honorable, respectful, honest, and just. We know what it is like to struggle for the right to vote and equal pay for equal work. We know what it's like to be relegated to second class citizenship, yet we struggle to achieve full citizenship. In spite of all of this, we have never lost our capacity to move with certainty to accomplish a task and fulfill a goal. We refuse to take "no" for an answer because we believe in ourselves, in each other, in God Almighty. Although there have been efforts to destroy the black family since we arrived on American soil, African American women have remained steadfast. We have understood that faith in God allows us to see the invisible and do the impossible. When institutions degraded us, our faith in God elevated us. When governments oppressed us, our faith in God helped to liberate us. When men violated us, our faith in God comforted us. We have understood that we were put here for a purpose and that purpose is to serve this present age, our calling to fulfill.

In the words of Laura B. Randolph:

Black women have always known what it takes to move mountains. With uncommon courage, unparalleled creativity, unwavering commitment, we don't know the meaning of "can't" and have never accepted the concept of impossible. Generation after generation, from Mary McLeod Bethune to Fannie Lou Hamer to Rosa Parks to Coretta Scott King, black women have always made a way out of no way. For centuries, with nothing more than wit, and will, faith, and foresight, black women have transformed tragedy into triumph, converted burdens into blessings, and some-how, some way, made something out of nothing.

Yes, because we stayed focused on the Lord, historically we as African American women have had staying power. To-day, however, it seems as if some of us have gotten off track. Our focus is on what men and women think about us rather than what God has called us to do. But if we don't have faith in God, setbacks and disappointments will seem unbearable and unconquerable. We will be tempted to throw up our hands and give up on ourselves. However, if we focus on God we will be able to rise above any challenge or controversy we might face.

Often, it is the attitude one has that determines the stay-ing power. A woman who feels good about herself is more apt to hold out when adversity sets in, so it is important to de-velop a positive state of mind. A person's success or lack thereof is not just tied to her ability but to whether or not she believes she can. For "as a [person] thinketh, so is [she]."

Our society and our roles and responsibilities as women are rapidly changing. This is why it is so important to have something that is sure, steady, unalterable, and definite. We need something that fire cannot consume, water cannot erode, and political forces cannot corrupt. We need a solid rock and a sure foundation.

In all of our strategies, God has always been that solid rock, leading us, guiding us, directing us, supporting us, in-spiring us, and loving us. Without God, we could do nothing.

I have always heard little quirky sayings about women,

such as "You can always tell a beautiful woman, but you can't tell her much" or "There's only one way to handle a woman. The trouble is nobody knows what it is." But I share the opinion of Victor Hugo, who said, "Men have sight; women have insight." I agree with Ralph Waldo Emerson who said, "A sufficient measure of civilization is the influence of women."

Mothers, daughters, aunts, grandmothers, sisters—in every way, women have made a difference. Throughout the Bible, we read about great women inspired by God. We read of the faith of Sarah, the courage of Esther, the determination of Ruth, the commitment of Priscilla, the compassion of Mary, and the wisdom of Martha. History is replete with accounts of the contributions of women.

Certainly there are those of us today who have made tremendous contributions to the African American family and community. But we must be careful not to allow society to divide us. Over the years, our society has perpetuated the myth that women who remain in the home and devote themselves full time to raising their children don't work, but nothing could be further from the truth. Not only are they working full time, they're working overtime. We cannot afford the false battle of the professional versus the domestic woman, the learned versus the unlearned woman. God made us all and all of our roles are equally important. Homemaker, doctor, lawyer, minister, politician, teacher, business woman, or student—all of these roles are important. If we are going to save our families and community from corruption and erosion, we all have to pitch in.

As women we need a unifying vision. Without it, we will continue to sacrifice an entire generation to crime, ignorance, and deception. Many of our youth are searching for meaning and direction, yet we've been guilty of giving them things but not ourselves. We've given them cars so that they can drive us crazy and Walkmans so they can listen to explicit lyrics and learn the language of insult rather than the language of respect. We give them designer clothes so that they can look good on the outside when they are dying on the inside.

But what our children are saying to us is, "Help us, direct us, give us some guidance, some vision." Those of us who are quick to criticize them, though, must never forget who raised or didn't raise them. As the African proverb reminds us, "It takes an entire village [community] to raise a child." Therefore, whether or not they're biologically ours, what they know, we taught them; where they are, we brought them; and where they go, we must show them the way.

As black African American women, we must take on the special responsibility of addressing the problem of babies having babies in our communities. According to the Children's Defense Fund, every 104 seconds a black teenage girl becomes pregnant. Every eleven minutes a baby is born to a black teen mother who already has a child. As women, we must teach these young women that motherhood is not merely giving birth to a child but involves being willing and able to raise and instruct that child. Furthermore, we are called upon to address the fact that every sixty-nine seconds a black baby is born to an unmarried mother, helping to account for the more than 50 percent of households in the black community headed by women. For too long we have looked to others to take care of us; the time has come for us to take care of ourselves.

We should use the expertise and gifts of our sororities and other sisterhood organizations to educate, inform, direct, and guide the values of our young people. Our organizations must be more than social clubs. We must go into the communities, the churches, the girls' clubs, and youth groups, and conduct seminars, teach-ins, rap sessions, and symposiums. Our girls need not only to hear from a positive black woman but to see and experience a relationship with one.

No longer can we allow "Living Single" to be our prime time and church to be our some time. We must rediscover our roots and values.

For too long, our society has been based on the premise of "get all you can, by any means you can, as quickly as you can, and by stepping on whomever you can." As African American women, we must not fall prey to this. We must take our time and reach out to a young sister who needs just a little encouragement and a little assistance and make that difference in her life, for making a difference is what life is all about.

Many of our young sisters, especially our teenage mothers, simply need someone to believe in them. Usually their self-esteem is low and their view of the future is hopeless. Our challenge is to restore that feeling of self-worth and that glimmer of hope, for without hope, it is virtually impossible to make it.

What so many mothers, aunts, and grandmothers who never went to college, and who never lived in the suburbs or townhouses, have been known to give to their children is hope: no matter how bad it is, it is going to be better tomorrow; no matter how dilapidated our apartment, one day we will have a clean place to lay our heads. Our foreparents were able to keep hope alive. They taught us that it's not what you have that counts, but what you do with what you do have. This is the hope that needs to be restored in our young people, in our girls who have surrendered that hope.

We must teach our younger sisters that it is important not only to be themselves, but to be their best selves; that they can never be satisfied with mediocrity but must always reach for the stars. For when a woman is her best self, mountains become molehills, stumbling blocks become stepping stones, valleys become pathways, the unreachable becomes obtainable, the impossible becomes practical, the unforeseen becomes visible, and the crooked is straightened out.

In each of us is a sleeping giant of potential waiting to be awakened and energized. When we seek to become our best selves, there always seems to be somebody trying to hold us back. Someone will give us one hundred reasons why it cannot be done. Someone will tell us how it will never work. But I operate from the premise that "If my mind can conceive it, and my heart can believe it, then I can achieve it." No one knows what we can do better than us, so we mustn't quit just because it is hard, or difficult, or the resources aren't available. We mustn't focus on the obstacles but on the opportunities.

When we are our best selves, we would rather have a hand than a hand-out, rather be empowered than imprisoned by bad habits. When we are our best selves, we walk with new dignity and renewed purpose; we smile in the face of adversity; and we confront those forces that would degrade us and rob us of our womanhood. Deep down in us, we know that there is the courage of Harriet Tubman, the patience of Mary

Church Terrell, the eloquence of Mary McLeod Bethune, the vision of Coretta Scott King, the commitment of Marian Wright Edelman, the creativity of Debbie Allen, the oratory of Shirley Chisholm, and the love of Mother Teresa. We are an unstoppable force.

YOUTH
AND
NONVIOLENCE

Probably the most talked about subjects when it comes to youth are violence and crime. Everybody wants to know what can be done to rescue our youth from the reality of violence and crime. As a result, all across this nation, especially in the inner cities where violence and crime rates are the worst, antiviolence campaigns and programs have been started. The efforts that have been most effective are the ones that involved youth in the planning and the implementation. I am certainly not suggesting that youth be left alone to solve the problems, but I am suggesting that young people be an integral part of whatever it is that we as adults try to sell them.

It is no secret that the greatest influence on youth is their peers. In fact, my work with different youth groups revealed that peers are the greatest influence on young people, followed by, in order: rap music, the media, parents, and school. This suggests that young people today have a tremendous amount of responsibility when it comes to changing the minds, attitudes, hearts, and environments of other youth. We adults can give guidance and direction, but young people will have to be the ones to get real with their peers and show them a better way of living.

Since violence and crime are realities that few youth can escape and which most want to do something about, I want to talk about what young people can do to lessen the violence and crime they witness or experience. But first I want to share some information gathered by the Children's Defense Fund:

Every day, 1,295 teenagers give birth, 40 give birth to their third child.

Every day, 689 babies are born to women who have had inadequate prenatal care.

Every day, 27 children die from poverty.

Every day, 135,000 children bring a gun to school, 30 are wounded by guns, and 10 die from guns.

Every day, 34,285 people lose jobs.

Every day, 1,512 teenagers drop out of school, amounting to at least one teenager per minute of every hour of every day.

("Children 1990: A Report and Briefing Book and Action Primer")

These statistics suggest that the needs and concerns of young people are being ignored and neglected. The longer they are ignored and neglected, the worse the situation will become. Young people will do whatever it takes to get the attention that they are not getting. My father, Dr. King, used to say that "violence is the voice of the unheard." It is no surprise, then, that young people who have been ignored or neglected act out in violent and criminal ways. This behavior is a young person's way of saying, "I've got a problem and I need you to help me with the problem." The problem could be a lack of love at home, poor living conditions, limited money to keep food on the table and a decent roof over their head, drug and/or alcohol abuse in the home. Whatever the case, to help free someone from these circumstances, one cannot use violence. Too many young people think that if they arm themselves with an AK-47, an Uzi, or 9mm, they can protect themselves from all of the violence and crime, when the truth is that all of the AK-47s, Uzis, and 9mm's in the world won't get rid of the conditions and circumstances that precipitate violence. Together we need to form a plan of action that will use people power. Guns don't change things; people change things.

115
.

This is what the philosophy of nonviolence that we call Kingian nonviolence is all about. In Kingian nonviolence, you start from the belief that violence and crime are signs that something needs fixing in society or in a person's immediate environment. The way to fix it is not with more violence but with methods designed to bring about positive change. Usually the problems that any one person faces are bigger than that person; it is not a personal problem but a societal one, too big for one individual to take on alone. The individual needs help because one person is likely to look at a problem in society and do nothing about it just because they think that one person can't make a difference. But if that same person were to reach out to other people who are concerned about the problem, then there would be enough people to address it. Nonviolent social change happens when people come to-gether to work on a problem that is bigger than any one of them. It is called nonviolent social change because people bring about change; weapons of destruction do not. The true power to change your community is in the hands of people, not in the guns. Therefore, if you, the youth, want to change the situation in your community, you are going to have to reach out to other youth and work together as an organiza-tion. That's why I don't have a problem with the notion of gangs because there's a lot of people power in gangs. But gangs need to learn to use their power constructively, not de-structively. If enough of you understand nonviolence and are willing to commit to it, then perhaps you ought to join these gangs and turn them around.

A few years ago, a group of high school students in Atlanta got together because they were tired of all the violence in their schools. They created an organization to monitor the violence in and around the high school and to report it to the necessary people. They also started after-school tutorial pro-grams to help those with academic problems. Another group of young people at a high school in Atlanta walked out of school to express their dissatisfaction over the fact that out-side agitators could come into their school and stir up vio-lence and conflict. As a result, school officials enhanced security precautions at the school.

I share these stories to emphasize that there is power in numbers and that people working together in a common cause can achieve much more than one concerned person. Dr. King's nonviolent philosophy was effective in bringing about change because it brought together people power. That's what movement means.

Once you bring together other young people, you must have an agenda. The plan of action should have five steps:

1. *Identify or recognize a problem.* This is important because you are dealing with so many problems that unless you focus on just one or two you will lose a lot of people. I have discovered that if people are given too many issues to focus on they get frustrated and will usually give up. Young people get restless when too much is coming at them, so choose no more than one or two issues. If you have two issues, break the group into subgroups to take on the different problems.

2. *Analyze the issue.* This is a critical step in changing anything, for if you do not understand the issue, you might go half-cocked in the wrong direction or put the cart before the horse. Find out as much as you can about the issue so that you know the who, what, where, and why. For example, if your issue is high school dropouts, then you especially need to understand who drops out, when and why they drop out. In many minority communities, young people typically drop out because the curriculum doesn't reflect their multicultural interests. This means that if you decide to put together an after-school program, tutoring is not enough. You need some culturally relevant sessions, or you will be left wondering, where did I go wrong? Many programs in our inner cities fall short because people don't look at the whole problem. This

second step can be summed up in these words: *it's always good to know what you're getting into before you get into it.*

3. **Look at the options that are available to you.** This helps you keep a sense of perspective. It's easy to talk about all of the wonderful ways to solve a problem, but if those wonderful ways are not available, then you've talked yourself into a big ball of frustration. You need to look at what's practical and reasonable. You may want to start an alternative school for high school dropouts. But if you don't have the money and the properly trained and certified adults, the school is just a good idea, a dream deferred. This third step, then, can be summarized in the following words: *get real about what you can and what you can't do.*

4. **Make your plan of action according to the options that are available.** When Dr. King and others planned for the boycott of the buses in Montgomery, it would have been unreasonable for them to demand that most of the white bus drivers be fired in favor of hiring more black bus drivers. Such a demand would have been rejected, and black people's expectations might have been raised only to turn into disappointment. A lot of headaches and energy can be saved if you do what you can do within your own power and leave the rest to someone else. *You can only do what you can do.*

5. **Implement the plan of action.** This means putting it into action. This is where the rubber hits the road. Talk is cheap unless the talk becomes action. Many programs never make it out of the conference room or the classroom because people fail to take action. Remember that it's not what you talk about but what you do with what you talk about that will make your communities better places to live.

Now, allow me to explain to you how these steps make you an agent for nonviolent social change. First, Kingian nonviolence is a philosophy that seeks to preserve rather than to destroy life. The five steps are a positive and constructive way to handle issues rather than a destructive way. Instead of people being destroyed, problems are solved. The focus, then, is on the problem and not the people causing the problem. Any bitterness, frustration, or anger is directed toward resolving the problem. Nothing is wrong with anger if you direct it in the right manner. These five steps are the avenue for expressing the pent-up emotions of young people. I believe this because studies have shown that if you keep young people focused on problem solving, on doing things that are constructive, there is less chance of that young person getting into trouble.

This brings me to the next point about Kingian nonviolence. It is active, not passive, as many have thought. In Kingian nonviolence you don't just sit back and allow things to happen, but you do something about them. A passive person does nothing about a problem or issue but talk about it. The five steps are a way of doing something about a problem.

Some people might tell you that unless you are armed with weapons, ready to do battle, you can't be serious about changing things. Some people believe that freedom only comes through the barrel of a gun. However, in Kingian nonviolence weapons of destruction are prohibited because your goal is freedom and understanding, and freedom and understanding don't mean anything if you've got a lot of dead people and nothing has changed. That's why in Kingian nonviolence we say that you are passive only in the physical sense of the word, because you refuse to destroy people and property in the process. All of your energy is devoted to a plan of action that seeks change, not destruction.

I feel that the reason why so many young people and rap artists are preoccupied with the realities of violence and crime in "the hood" is because they have failed to understand that you don't have to wait until something goes down to do something. You can keep trouble from happening. It's called being proactive rather than reactive. If more young people were to get involved in improving their communities, then we wouldn't have to take the easy way out when a crisis happens. Violence is always the easy way out because you don't have to think and you don't have to work hard. When you engage in violence you just react to the situation. When you are not already involved in a plan of action to resolve an issue, when the problem gets worse you just become mad, and mad people always destroy things. In Kingian nonviolence, you don't get mad, you get smart. Therefore, by talking about the issues that concern young people and coming up with plans of action, you are a step ahead of many of your peers. You are doing the smart thing. The answers to the problems you face are in your hands. Remember, don't get mad, get smart; it just might save your life and mine.

A WORLDHOUSE BUILT
ON A FOUNDATION
OF CULTURAL DIVERSITY

I have so many warm memories of my years as a Girl Scout. For me and millions of other girls, scouting was not only about fun and enjoyment, it was a formative, character-building experience as well.

In his book, *Where Do We Go from Here? Chaos or Community,* my father, Martin Luther King Jr., outlined his vision for the world. He compared the predicament of humanity to that of a large family of diverse individuals who were forced to live together under one roof. "We have inherited a large house," he said, "a great 'worldhouse' in which we have to live together—black and white, Easterner and Westerner, Gentile and Jew, Catholic and Protestant, Muslim and Hindu." He said this is "a family unduly separated by ideas, culture, and interests, who . . . must learn somehow to live with each other in peace."

My father envisioned a worldhouse where all people could share in the wealth of the earth. In his worldhouse, international disputes would be resolved by peaceful conflict resolution instead of military power. In the worldhouse, hunger and homelessness would not be tolerated because international standards of human decency would not allow it. In the worldhouse, racial conflict would be replaced by a new spirit of interracial brotherhood and sisterhood, trust would prevail over fear and hatred, and a beloved community of peace with justice would reign supreme. He believed that nonviolence was the only way to bring the worldhouse into being.

In sharing this vision, we don't just tolerate multicultural diversity; we celebrate it even as we recognize our common humanity. We don't surrender our group identities; we weave them into a cooperative and mutually supportive framework. Multicultural unity is not only a way we can live together but also a powerful tool for personal, social, and political transformation.

Racism, anti-Semitism, and other forms of ethnic and cultural hatred flourish in a climate of cultural isolation and suspicion. We have eliminated segregation in public facilities such as restaurants and public transportation, thanks to the American civil rights movement. But we still have a long way to go before we purge the segregation in the human heart.

I don't believe this will happen unless we take responsibility for it and make it happen. As Martin Luther King Jr. said, "Racial understanding is not something that we find, but something that we must create. Our ability to work together, to understand each other, will not be found ready made; it must be created by the fact of contact." That's why programs that actively promote interracial and intercultural understanding are essential if we are to make real the dream of a nation unified in brotherhood and sisterhood.

It is important to understand that the civil rights movement of the 1950s and 1960s was not only about freedom for black Americans. It was also about the liberation of white Americans, of poor and rich people. The civil rights movement freed segregationists from the psychological burdens of their self-delusions and false sense of superiority, which impeded their spiritual growth and prevented the nation from progressing toward our true destiny. America can never realize its magnificent promise until all citizens are able to share equally in the promise of equality.

The rebellions that occurred in Los Angeles, Atlanta, San Francisco, and other cities following the Rodney King verdict were, in part, a product of the continuing estrangement of black, white, Asian, and Hispanic youth. Any type of racial polarization that erupts in violence represents a failure of our churches, temples, and mosques, our schools and community organizations, as well as a failure of moral leadership in too many American families. Religious leaders, the schools, community and service organizations, the private sector, including both business and labor, must all do more to create, sponsor, and support programs that promote multicultural understanding and cooperation. We have to be together and spend some time together before we can truly live together as brothers and sisters.

We must also find a way to put an end to the corrosive poverty and deprivation that provides such a fertile ground for riots and other community disturbances.

I don't think we can talk about leadership in a vacuum, because leadership is so much more complex in a multicultural society. Leadership in America, more than any other nation, is about building consensus among people of vastly different backgrounds. If we can find a way to live together, we can lead the world into the twentieth century.

The Girl Scouts is one of the few nationwide organizations that has provided leadership training for young women. One of the reasons the world is in such a mess is because every nation has suppressed women from full participation in its political and economic institutions. Women are 53 percent of the population of the United States but account for only 6 percent of the 535 members of the U.S. Congress. And you can count the number of women heading Fortune 500 companies on one hand.

There are compelling economic as well as moral reasons for more leadership development programs for girls and women. I don't see how we can afford much longer the luxury of writing off the creative contributions of more than half of the population, if the United States is going to be competitive in the global marketplace in the 1990s. Few investments the public and private sector can make in the 1990s will be more cost-effective than those that support leadership development programs for minorities and women.

Such an investment is all the more crucial to America's future in light of the recent series of U.S. Supreme Court decisions undermining affirmative action programs for women and minorities. The high court's assault on affirmative action provides comfort to no one except a few contractors and ideologues. No matter what the legal status of affirmative action, however, the nation's corporate community can exceed the requirements of the law by accelerating their commitment to train, hire, and promote women and African Americans and other minorities. With such a commitment we could achieve something approaching equal playing ground for all Americans by the millennium.

So I appeal to those in corporate settings to become activists in the struggle against discrimination. One can set the highest standards of equal opportunity by urging one's company to hire more African Americans and other minority men and women and to set up training programs and scholarships for disadvantaged young people. The variety of initiatives that can be employed in the struggle for equal opportunity in the private sector is limited only by one's imagination and commitment.

If we as a nation are serious about setting the pace as leaders in the future, then there is something important that we can learn from the Japanese. For the Japanese, education is of paramount importance.

Our leaders pay mere lip service to the importance of education. When it is time to fund education, Uncle Sam and the state and local governments become cheapskates. Our politicians lavish billions of dollars on weapons of destruction, but they talk about fiscal responsibility when the subject of funding educational programs is raised. Somehow we must make them understand that education is as much of a national security issue for America's survival as is military power. If we win the arms race but lose the education race our national security will be severely compromised.

Accepting this commitment will not be an inexpensive undertaking. We are going to have to train and hire more teachers in order to make smaller classes, and pay them better. We are going to have to build more schools and outfit them with better facilities and equipment, and we are going to have to provide more financial assistance to needy students. This will require painful choices about spending priorities and taxes. But if we do not act, the next generation may not have a chance to correct our mistakes. We, the people, must make it clear to our leaders that our votes depend on their facing this issue.

Let us resolve to make concern for others the first law of our lives, so that we can put an end to the epidemic of violence that is destroying our communities. Instead of tolerating violent gangs in the ghettos and barrios of our cities, let us train and organize young people for nonviolent conflict resolution. Instead of shaking our heads in disbelief at incidents of child neglect and abuse, let us work for the day when we have concerned and committed block parents in every street and housing project in the nation. Instead of merely lamenting epidemic drug abuse, let us forge a national partnership of business, government, religious, and community-based organizations to educate young people about drug abuse, and let us provide them with job training, especially entrepreneurial development, and educational opportunities so that they can have some real hope for a better future.

This is what we have tried to create at the Martin Luther King, Jr. Center for Nonviolent Social Change. The King center exists to preserve Martin Luther King Jr.'s legacy and dream. But we are not just about celebrating the past. We intend to carry forward this legacy into the future and to educate and train as many people as possible in his philosophy and strategy of nonviolence so that they can apply these lessons to address the crises we are currently facing and those we will be facing in the years ahead.

The center is committed to Martin Luther King Jr.'s dream of a beloved world community in which people of all races, religions, and nations are united by a common bond of love and goodwill. We want to help prepare people to create a world without war, racism, hunger, poverty, or deprivation, a world without prejudice and discrimination.

Instead of the arms race, we want to lift up the human race. Instead of investing in more weapons of death and destruction, we want to see investments in education and economic development, so that all people are free to realize their full human potential.

This is ambitious. But God did not put us here to dream small dreams and perform insignificant deeds. The struggle to fulfill Martin Luther King Jr.'s dream of the beloved community will demand all of our resources of courage, dedication, and, yes, sacrifice. But now is not the time for hesitation. Now is not the time for uncertainty. Now is not the time for indecision.

But now is the time to move forward in a unified nonviolent coalition to fulfill the promise of democracy. Now is the time to make real the dream of freedom and justice. And now is the time to stand up for national unity, peace, and world sisterhood and brotherhood.

THE
STUFF
INSIDE

It has been said that if you want power, seek knowledge. And yet some of the most knowledgeable people possessed power that became destructive. Many lives have been drastically altered because of people who did not understand the power of misguided knowledge.

Adolf Hitler was a highly intelligent individual, and yet he used his knowledge to cause millions of senseless murders. Alfred Nobel founded the Nobel Prize for Peace and yet he created dynamite, which has claimed hundreds of innocent lives, and his theories led to the development of nuclear weapons, which are and have been more destructive than dynamite.

Many great minds have been utilized on projects that have led to social destruction rather than to social uplift. The tragedy is that we do not yet understand the relationship between knowledge and good old common sense. History teaches us that some of the intellectually brightest people have been the most destructive, while some of the less intelligent have proved to be the most constructive.

In the words of Dr. Benjamin Elijah Mays, former president of Morehouse College:

> There is no guarantee [that] when we train a person's mind, we will train his heart; no guarantee that when we increase a person's knowledge we will increase his goodness. There is no necessary correlation between knowledge and goodness. A person can know the truth and deliberately lie; see the good and deliberately choose evil; see the light and deliberately walk in darkness; see the high road beckoning to him and deliberately choose the low road.

This statement affirms that knowledge alone is not enough. All the knowledge in the world won't guarantee a life of security; neither will it guarantee a successful life. Therefore, we must seek more than a mere education. We must search for vision and purpose.

In order for life to have meaning and for a person to be truly successful, one must have a sense of commitment. No doubt there are many who feel that they are committed and are aware of others who are committed as well. The real question, though, is "Who are you committed to?" Some people are committed to power itself, some to position, others to prestige, and still others to just making money. But I have come to realize that, in John Wesley's words, true commitment means "doing all the good you can, in all the places you can, to all the people you can, for as long as you ever can."

There are many who think that just because they are smarter and have more business savvy, they are better than everyone else. My father made a profound statement challenging this kind of attitude: "You don't have to have a college degree to serve, you don't have to make your subject and verb agree to serve. You don't have to know Einstein's theory of relativity or the second theory of thermodynamics to serve. All you need is a heart full of grace and a soul generated by love." A person is great when that person is committed to serve.

If our lives are to be meaningful and complete, then all of us, no matter how young or old, are called upon to have a commitment that extends beyond mere financial security. The challenge is to have a three-dimensional life commitment—serving self, others, and God.

Many say that serving self can be a selfish aspiration, and it is, if it is your only commitment and goal in life. But there is a commitment to self that is necessary if we wish to lead a wholesome and rewarding life. This kind of commitment to self means knowing who you are in total. This is of supreme importance because too many people are living their lives solely to please others. It seems that many of us are more concerned about what others think and feel about us than what we think and feel about ourselves. We bow too easily to peer pressure and societal standards of what's important and how to fit in, and we are losing our identity in the process.

I remember someone telling me when I was a teenager, "It's better to be alone and be yourself than be in a crowd and be someone else." At the time I didn't quite get the point. But later on, I heard someone mimic an elderly lady who said: "It's hard enough being who you is, let alone who you ain't."

It is difficult trying to be true to who we are. That's why it's important that we not expend energy on trying to be like someone who we really can't be anyway. We should focus on discovering what God has called us to do and doing it in such a way that no person living or yet to be born could duplicate its effect. It has nothing to do with how good we look on the outside. It doesn't matter how much money we make, what kind of clothes we wear, what type of car we drive or house we live in; but, as the elders have said, "It's what you do with what you do have." This attitude comes only from realizing that we are not defined by what is on the outside of us, but by what is on the inside.

This reminds me of a story that the great concert singer Marian Anderson told. She talked about a little boy in a park who had a great big, white balloon. While playing around he accidentally tripped and fell, losing his great big, white balloon. After watching the wind take it and lift it into the sky, he spotted a vendor in the park who had many other different colored balloons—black, brown, red, and yellow balloons. The little boy ran over to the vendor and said, "Sir, I had a great big, white balloon and I lost it. If I had had a brown balloon, would it have risen up into the sky as high as my white balloon did?" The vendor said, "Yes." "How about a red one?" And the vendor said, "Yes." "Well, what if I had had a black balloon, would it have risen into the sky as high as my white balloon did?" The vendor said, "Of course, son, it's not the color of the balloon—it's the stuff inside."

Indeed, some of that stuff on the inside is the gifts, talents, abilities, and knowhow that God has given to all of us. None of us is talentless.

It is imperative that we identify and develop our own unique and special gifts. Unless we do this we will not be able to give because one cannot give unless one has something inside to give. What it ultimately boils down to is a commitment to love one's self, which is most important because we cannot truly love others until we love ourselves. And if we love ourselves we will not do things that are harmful and destructive to ourselves, like abusing drugs and alcohol. When we have a healthy self-love we will not allow anyone to abuse us or lead us in the wrong direction.

Loving one's self is not easy. It takes a lot of energy and effort to develop healthy self-love that is not an arrogant, boastful, better-than-thou love.

What is healthy self-love? It requires looking at one's self honestly, as if facing a mirror, then getting naked by stripping away the attitudes, defenses, and illusions one might have about one's self. It requires coming to grips with our needs and recognizing those things that motivate us. Moreover, it means accepting our strengths and capabilities while at the same time acknowledging our shortcomings and fears.

Once this is accomplished, then we must be able to look at ourselves and say truthfully, I'm okay. I like me. I have something to offer in this world. But we can't stop here. We must embrace all of the positives and the negatives about ourselves and commit to developing and molding ourselves in ways that will be beneficial to our well-being and positive growth. It's a commitment that can't be accomplished in a couple of days or a few seminars. Some people spend a lifetime and never find out who they truly are. But discovering and developing the stuff inside of us is necessary if the world is to be a better place.

Many dreams and inventions and discoveries are buried in the cemeteries, because many people stopped short of developing the potential within them. Maybe they didn't think they had anything to offer; or what they had to offer wasn't good enough. But each of us brings something to the table besides an appetite.

Douglas Mallock put it best when he said, "If you can't be a pine on the top of the hill, be a scrub in the valley, but be the best scrub by the side of the rill. Be a bush, if you can't be a tree. If you can't be a highway, just be a trail. If you can't be the sun, just be a star. For it isn't by size that you win or fail. Be the best of whatever you are."

So many people have fallen prey to the status quo, and as a result we are some of the unhealthiest people in the world. I like to tell people that if you are not around to enjoy success, then what is it all worth? The Bible says, "What good is it for a [person] to gain the whole world, and yet lose or forfeit [their] very self?" (Luke 9:25) In other words, it doesn't make sense to commit one's self to a job or profession just to make mo' money if the reward is death (spiritual, mental, emotional, or physical). We will not be any good for ourselves or anybody else.

Right now, the number one killer of all Americans is heart disease, which is not brought on just by genetically acquired hypertension, but by stress. In fact, many illnesses and diseases have their origin in stress, because over time stress breaks down the immune system. Therefore, it's time that we start committing just as much time to taking care of ourselves as we do to our jobs and careers. When we don't make this kind of commitment to ourselves, then we are really being selfish because we will end up being no good not only for ourselves but for others as well.

Second, if our lives are to be complete and our success great, then we must be committed to more than self. We must be committed to others. Some people call this a commitment to serve humanity.

Contrary to what many might think or may have been taught, we do not live merely for self-gratification. In a real sense the main reason we spend time preparing ourselves is so that we can help nurture the communities in which we live. All of us are here on planet earth to make a difference and help one another along the way, and we will have to give an account of the space we occupy. To build a life of riches without being affected by the millions of people who suffer from social and economic destitution is a breach of our contract with humanity. Indeed, as John Donne said, "No man is an island, entire of itself; every man is a piece of the continent, a part of the main."

It is no mere accident that in our society today people are afraid of each other, and trust is at an all-time low. For a long time now, many people have lived by the philosophy, "It's just me, myself, and I." Because most people have been looking out just for number one, many people have fallen through the cracks and become burdens rather than blessings to society.

The reason that violence and crime have gripped and captivated our society is not because people are violent or criminal by nature, but because people are expressing their frustration and anger with the conditions in which they have been forced to live in such a wealthy nation. We can't glamorize the "lifestyles of the rich and famous" to economically deprived people and tell them that if you just work hard you can have this lifestyle, when the real truth is that no matter how hard you work, a capitalistic system is not designed to reward everybody the same. It is designed to have upper, middle, and lower class people. So where does this leave people? It leaves those at the bottom with the choice to beg, borrow, or steal, and even kill.

Does this mean that we should continue to arm ourselves with more guns? No! It just means that those of us who have more must be willing to share more. This doesn't mean that one has to relinquish everything one earns, or merely give a handout. No! Many people who are in socially and economically deprived situations don't want a handout, they want a hand up, a helping hand. To be or not to be poor is the question. Most would choose not to be poor. The best way we can help poor people is not to be one of them but to help them. That's why I encourage everyone to set time aside weekly to perform community service.

It's time out for the attitude "I've got mine, you've got to get yours." No matter how high up the ladder we go, there is always room to reach back and pull another brother or sister up with us. The best way to pull others up is not by merely feeding them a fish for a day, but by teaching them how to fish so that they can feed themselves for a lifetime. This is what breeds true character in another person. And if there is any-thing that we need more of in this society, it is not more rich people but more people with character.

Character is more than money in the bank, more than a prized possession. Character is what gives us that staying power when times get tough. It's what keeps people from los-ing their heads and sense of somebodiness. You can take a per-son who has wealth and no character, and over time he will blow the wealth or blow himself away. Or you can take a per-son who has no wealth but who has character, and over time he will flourish and reach his full potential. A person without character is like a boat without a sail.

Right now in many of our communities, we have some boats without sails because too many people are stuck in un-fair and unjust circumstances and they can't seem to make it out of the storms of economic and social deprivation. This is why it is important that each of us do more than just give to the least of these, but that we spend quality time helping them discover and develop their full potential.

It is important to develop a strong sense of self so that we can contribute something to the betterment of our commu-nities. I realize that no one person can solve all the problems and help all the people, but there is something that each of us can do to make our own community at least a little better.

None of us can afford to sit around and wait for something to happen or sit back and hold our hands, hoping and praying that somebody will deliver us from the evil and injustices of our time. That somebody has to be each of us. Instead of spending far too much time making a living, we must commit ourselves to making a life for ourselves and our young people. This means that we need more than faith that will move mountains, rather, we need faith that will move us to do the things that need to be done to better humanity.

Finally, if our life is to be super-fulfilling and our quest for greatness complete, then the most important stuff that must be inside us is a commitment to God. This commitment will cause us to transcend our mere physical reality and make us realize that we have a higher calling than just sitting back and living off the fat of the land. This commitment to God will give us the faith and courage to take on any injustice or problem we're faced with. A commitment to God causes us to keep our eyes on our goals without giving up because we realize that God has not called us to be successful but to be faithful. Therefore, even when the statistics are against you, even when doors are shut in your face, even when the outcome looks bleak, you can continue to push ahead and focus on the positive rather than the negative because you realize that God doesn't desire to see His children fail. When you are committed to God you never become satisfied or comfortable with the way things are because you recognize that there is always more that needs to be done, and you are willing to do it no matter what the cost.

Only a person who has a relationship with God will ultimately discover his or her purpose and reason for living. Without this commitment, a person wanders aimlessly, perpetually searching for success and happiness but never really finding it. When you believe that God is the one who created all of humanity, then you allow God to be your guide in this misguided world.

There's a story about a girl who wanted to have her

137

mother play Nintendo with her. One day while her mother was reading the newspaper the daughter interrupted, insisting that her mother come and play Nintendo with her. The mother agreed to play with the daughter later. However, the daughter insisted that the mother stop reading her newspaper and play Nintendo now. By this time the mother had noticed a picture of the world in the paper. She tore it into pieces, gave it to her daughter, and encouraged her to go and put the pieces back together; when her daughter did that, then she would play with her. The daughter went to her room and proceeded to put the pieces together. After a few minutes, she returned to her mother with the picture of the world pieced together. The mother was stunned. She wanted to know how the daughter had put the pieces back so quickly. The daughter informed her that she saw a picture of a woman on the other side of the paper. When she put the woman together, the world came back together.

As we continue on our life journeys we must not lose sight of our commitment to self, others, and God. Too many people are trying to save the world, or they are just trying to save themselves, but we are challenged to not only get ourselves together but to help at least one other person get himself or herself together. Then the world in which we live will come together. It will not be easy, but, "If God be for us, who can be against us?" (Rom. 8:31)

HOW TO DEAL
WITH ·
THE MIDNIGHT HOUR

The midnight hour is a difficult period in a person's life. It could be the loss of a loved one, the loss of personal health, the loss of a child to drugs or a gang. It could be the loss or the lack of a loving relationship. It could be the loss or the lack of financial security. Whatever the case, there are those who, when their midnight hour comes, lose hope. They become so caught up in their situation that they fail to see any options that might allow them to move beyond it. This is when you have a dead-end hope.

But then there are those for whom the midnight hour is a time for decision making, for exercising one's faith, and not a time to become paralyzed. The story of Paul and Silas is certainly an example of exercising one's faith; for at the midnight hour, Paul and Silas, though bound in jail, looked beyond their circumstances. They could have become embittered, angered, or depressed about being placed in jail. They could have protested the action as an injustice that they didn't deserve. Paul and Silas did something that was ultimately more powerful. They armed themselves by calling upon the power of God.

We are now in a midnight hour. When the number one cause of death among young African American males is homicide, it's midnight. When every 104 seconds a black teenage girl becomes pregnant, it's midnight. When 60 percent of marriages inside and outside the body of Christ end in divorce, it's midnight. When a young child can find more love and concern in a close-knit gang than in a healthy, wholesome family, it's midnight. When many mothers are raising sons and daughters alone, it's midnight. When fathers, sons, and brothers can't support their family or themselves with a decent-paying job, so they turn to drugs, it's midnight.

The question is, what are we going to do about it? How are we going to respond? There are those who have already responded with hopelessness. There are those who feel that it ain't going to get no better. There are those who have said that it's just the way it is. There are those who have even written the eulogy for an entire generation, who say we've lost a generation. There are those who have looked at the situation and concluded that there is nothing they can do about it. Well, believe it or not, they're all wrong.

There is good news. There is always a way to handle a midnight hour. Ephesians 6:11 tells us that we must arm ourselves with the whole armor of God. The problem is that we have been resorting to our own knowledge and strength to solve all of our problems. Think about it! We build more prisons to stop crime and yet crime increases. Oppressed and depressed people strike out violently at anything and anybody, and yet oppression still remains. Fearful citizens purchase guns to protect themselves, and yet robbery and aggravated assault and carjacking are on the rise. But the Bible I read says, "Not by might, nor by power, but by my Spirit, says the Lord of hosts." (Zech. 4:6)

Yes, if there ever was a time we needed the Lord, we sure do need Him now. No matter how big the situation or how overwhelming the circumstance, you should always keep in mind that "me and God are a majority." Paul and Silas certainly knew this. They were just two men against a Roman system that didn't like their preaching about the Lord and jailed them because of it. But at the midnight hour, they didn't lose it, like some of us do. They didn't panic. They didn't become paralyzed. They didn't cuss somebody out. They armed themselves with the power of God. They sought the Lord.

Well, how did they do this? Let's look at it a little closer. In Acts 16:25 it says, "At midnight, Paul and Silas were praying and singing praises to God." Now with all of the pain inflicted on Paul and Silas and the fact that they were imprisoned, they could have lost it. They could have given up hope of being released. But in spite of their situation, they were praying and praising God. How many of us can be found praying and praising God at a midnight hour? We serve a mighty God, an omnipotent—all-powerful—God. Nothing is too hard for God, whose power can deliver us out of our midnight hour. But it's not automatic. We can't just sit back and hope for God to deliver us. Faith without work is dead, and so we've got to activate the power. It says in 2 Chronicles 7:14, "If my people, who are called by my name, would humble themselves, pray, and seek my face, and turn from their wicked ways, then will I hear from heaven. I will forgive their sins and heal their land." It's an if-then proposition. If we seek God, then God will respond.

When Paul and Silas prayed and praised, it says in Acts 16:26, "And suddenly there was a great earthquake that shook the foundation of the prison, causing all the doors to open and everyone's chains to be loosed." Isn't it wonderful to know that, through prayer and praise, we can activate the presence and power of God in our lives? Because prayer and praise are both communications with God, let's examine them separately to better understand their importance.

I suggested that if we seek God, then God will answer. But it's not quite that simple. If you read the book of Acts, you will discover that Paul and Silas were praying men and this was not just some isolated plea for help. As it says in Luke 18:1, "Men ought always to pray and not faint." Ephesians 6:18 tells us to "pray always." Always means frequently and regularly. When people are faced with a midnight situation, we usually tell them to pray and everything will be all right. But if people don't pray or pray infrequently, we are misleading them into thinking that any time they're at a low, all they need to do is pray and God will deliver them. It isn't as if God is this cosmic bellhop that we can just call on when we get into trouble.

There is a reason that Ephesians 6:18 says pray always, for we are establishing a relationship with God when we pray.

And just as in any relationship, God wants to communicate constantly with us, not just when we get into trouble. Think about it. If the only time you reach out to me as a friend is when you need my help, then I'm apt to try to make myself unavailable as much as possible, or when I see you coming, I am going to turn away. Nobody wants to be used in this way. I'm sure that God gets tired of being called upon only when we get to low moments. Proverbs 3:6 says, "In all thy ways acknowledge Him, and He will direct thy path." If we are going to be Christians who are armed and dangerous, then in all our plans, decisions, and activities, we should acknowledge God. Every day we must live in a close, trusting relationship with God, always looking to Him for direction through prayer.

Paul and Silas were praying men. They had a constant prayer life, so when they sought God at the midnight hour, it was not something unusual or strange. It was easy for them to seek God while in prison because they had a relationship with God. Some of us, however, wait until life knocks us to our knees before we pray to God. I must inform you, though, that you can do more than pray after you have prayed, but you cannot do more than pray until you have prayed. In essence, a praying person is able to handle a midnight hour, whereas a non-praying or seldom-praying person worries constantly about his or her midnight hour. That's what Philippians 4:6–7 means when it says, "Be careful (or anxious) for nothing, but in everything by prayer and supplication with thanksgiving, let your request be made known unto God. And the peace of God, which passeth all understanding, shall keep your hearts and minds through Christ

Jesus." If you are always praying, when faced with a difficult battle in your life you don't lose it because you have assurance that God is working things out for you.

There is a poem about prayer that I think makes the point about always praying clear:

> I got up early one morning and rushed into the day.
> I had so much to accomplish that I didn't make time to pray.
> Problems just tumbling about me and heavier came each task.
> Why doesn't God help me? I wondered. He answered, you didn't ask.
> I wanted to see joy and beauty, but the day toiled on gray and bleak.
> I wondered why God didn't show me, He said, but you didn't seek.
> I tried to come into God's presence, I used all my keys at the lock.
> God gently chided: my child, you didn't knock.
> I woke up early this morning and paused before entering the day.
> I had so much to accomplish that I took time to pray.

Many of us are like the person in the poem. If I were to take a survey to determine how much of our lives we devote to prayer, I am certain that few of us would be able to admit to a daily prayer life; most of us would have to admit to a sporadic prayer life. All of the pulls and demands of life seem to leave little if any time in the day for prayer. But if we are going to handle all of the demands and battles that life presents us, then our prayer life must become a priority—if you make it a high priority, you will have a daily prayer life; if you make it a low priority, you will have a sporadic prayer life. There is a difference. James 5:16 tells us that "the effectual fervent prayer of the righteous availeth much." This means that a praying person is a powerful person.

What kind of power does the prayer life give us? For Paul and Silas, it was God interceding on their behalf through an earthquake. God can and sometimes does step in at a midnight hour and fix the situation or solve the problem. But sometimes our prayers render us stronger. Often we pray that a situation be removed or that deliverance or healing take place, but God allows the situation to remain and gives us strength to press on through. At one point, Paul prayed three times to have the thorn removed from his flesh, but instead of removing it, God gave him strength to live with it. Paul learned, "In whatsoever I am, therewith to be content." (Phil. 4:11) That's what I like about the advertising campaigns about AIDS. Instead of becoming overwhelmed by the disease, people with AIDS are learning to live with it.

No matter what midnight hour you're faced with, God can give you strength to live with it. Always remember that when you pray, God is working on your behalf. No matter what the midnight situation is, if you stay armed with prayer, God has a prescription for you. He will either remove it or give you the necessary strength to live through it. Therefore, rest in the knowledge that none of your prayers go unnoticed because through prayer you invoke God's power to work in your life.

145

An anonymous writer tells of a Christian woman who prayed:

> She asked for strength to do greater things, but was given infirmity that she might do better things.
> She asked for riches that she might be happy, but she was given poverty that she might be wise.
> She asked for power that she might have praise of women, but she was given weakness that she might fill the need of God.
> She had received nothing she had asked for, all that she hoped for.
> Her prayer seemed unanswered, but she was most blessed.

When we pray, God will provide us with an answer, although it may not be what we ask for. But prayer is more powerful when you add praises to God. It's not an either/or proposition; it's a both/and combination. Acts 16:25 says that at midnight Paul and Silas prayed and sang praises, or hymns. It was a combination of their prayers and praises that caused the earthquake to come. If you've been doing a lot of praying asking God for an answer or a solution to your midnight hour, try praising God, too. For when the praises go up, the blessings do indeed come down.

Praise is our expression of gratitude for what God has done, is doing, and will do. By focusing on God, we remove ourselves from any situation that might be preoccupying us. Thus, in prayer, often it's the situation that is the focus, but in praise, God becomes the focus. If something has you worried or stuck or down, try praising God; you might get some relief. Be careful, though, because you don't want to find yourself praising God for the mere purpose of getting your mind off a burdensome situation. That's called "praise because of." And that's not what we praise God for. In spite of their midnight hour, Paul and Silas sang praises to God.

The Bible doesn't say "praise the Lord if you feel like it" or "if things are going well for you" or "when all else fails"; it says, "Praise ye the Lord." In other words, we are commanded to praise the Lord. Praise is our way of giving God His due and recognizing Him for His goodness and mercy and power. It is in recognizing God for who He is that God recognizes us and blesses us more than we could ever imagine.

I always say to people that if you want to get out of your constipated way of living, then you've got to do more than cry out the blues to God. If you listen to most of the prayers and some of the Gospel music that we African Americans hold in high esteem, you would think that when God blesses, he overlooks us. We are a blues praying and blues singing people. But if we are going to receive power, and be armed and dangerous, then we've got to stop singing the blues all the time. It's time to praise the Lord. Psalm 100 says we must "enter into His gates with thanksgiving and into His courts with praise." In other words, we need to stop approaching God with complaints or asking for favors. Just as we want to hear good news, God wants to hear good news too. Why do you think the Bible says that "God inhabits the praises of His people?" God is at home with praise. He likes praise. He's comfortable with praise. He is familiar with praise. He lives and takes up residency in those who praise Him. In other words, God is attentive to the needs and concerns of those who praise Him.

No matter where we are or who is around, we need not be ashamed to offer prayer and praise to God. Paul and Silas were in prison praying and singing praises to God even though other prisoners were listening. There really is no ordained place to offer up prayer and praise to God. God is everywhere—omnipresent. We can invoke His power anywhere because the Bible says, "Wherever two or three are gathered in My name, there will I be also." It's time for us to arm ourselves with the power of God to help us handle our midnight hour.

A story is told about a certain cotton factory where there was a big card on the wall of each workroom that read, "If your threads get tangled, send for the foreman." One day, a new worker got her threads tangled, and she tried to disentangle them but only made them worse. Then she sent for the foreman. He came and looked. He said to her, "You have been doing this yourself." "Yes," she said. "But why did you not send for me according to instructions?" "I did my best," she said. "No, you did not," the foreman said. "Remember that doing your best is sending for me."

How many times have we, the people of God, tried to fix our situations alone and messed them up? God is waiting for us to send for him. Being armed and dangerous means we must "seek the Lord while He may be found, call upon Him while He is near." (Isa. 55:6) Prayer and praise are the avenues by which we can call upon the power of God. God has the power to unleash all kinds of possibilities in our lives. Like

Paul and Silas, we don't have to be down and out, we can be up and about.

You don't have to be down in despair—lift up your head. You don't have to be down in the dumps; you don't have to be down and discouraged—lift up your head. You don't have to be down and depressed; you don't have to be down and disturbed—lift up your head. You don't have to be down and defeated—lift up your head. The outlook may be dark and dreary, but the "up" looks so much better.

"Lift up your heads, O gates! and be lifted up, O ancient doors! that the King of glory may come in.

"Who is the King of glory? The Lord strong and mighty, the Lord mighty in battle!

"Lift up your heads, O gates!" (Ps. 24:7–9)

ACHIEVING EXCELLENCE
BY EMPOWERING YOURSELF
IN CHANGING TIDES

Many years ago George Benson recorded a song entitled "Everything Must Change." The lyrics suggest that even though we can't be sure of many things, one thing certain in life is change. No one is exempt from it. No one can deny its existence. No one can run and hide from it. It's everywhere. It's a natural fact of life that, once accepted as such, can prevent a lot of headaches and heartaches. Change is inevitable in our lives. We cannot do anything about it. However, if one wants to be empowered and in control when change happens, then one must take to heart those motivational words that tell us, "We cannot direct the wind, but we can adjust the sails."

Have you ever watched a piece of paper blowing in the wind? Its pattern of movement is unpredictable. It moves at the discretion of the wind. It's hard to catch because the wind controls and determines its destiny. The paper doesn't have the necessary strength, is too lightweight, to resist being affected by the wind.

Change in a person's life can be like the wind on the paper, if you don't have the necessary strength to withstand it. If you want to be in control when change comes along you must adjust your way of seeing, being, and doing. To be empowered in changing tides means that you must adjust your thinking and behavior in such a way that you will not be deterred from reaching your goals and achieving excellence. We cannot control all of the situations and circumstances that come our way in life, but we can control how we respond as a result of them. To be mediocre is to be affected when adversity comes, but to be excellent is to be effective.

Many are flustered when change comes because they aren't sure of themselves. I believe this is because some people do not yet know why they are here on the planet earth. If a person is going to achieve excellence, then understanding one's purpose or meaning in life is of utmost importance.

If you have not already done so, ask yourself, why am I here? What is my life work supposed to be? Once you do this, you will open the gateway to your soul and discover a wealth of information about yourself that you never knew.

How many of you are satisfied with where you are? Or, how many of you are doing what you've always wanted to do or dreamed of doing? Some people, I believe, are not satisfied with their place and accomplishments. And I'll tell you why. I have a friend who frequently got a headache or stomachache on Sunday nights. Once, after she had taken a long weekend vacation, I saw her at church the night before she was to return to work. She was slumped down in her seat and I asked her what was wrong. Guess what? She said, "I have a headache."

People are sick and tired of going to jobs that don't satisfy them because either the environment is nonsupportive or the possibility for promotion is bleak. Many are going to jobs that they hate, that don't challenge them, and that they get sick just thinking about. Migraine headaches are common among dissatisfied workers. While a person can stress out by over-doing it, a lot of people are stressed because they are unhappy or unfulfilled on the job. The problem is that many Americans are working in settings and under conditions that are highly competitive, adversarial, depressive, and even oppressive. Most people stay in those jobs that they don't like, that are not challenging them, because they feel, I have to—I don't have any other choice.

People who feel that they have to stay in a situation be-cause they don't see their way out are in bondage. It's called mental enslavement. When people can't find any excitement and enjoyment in what they are doing, there is no fun, merely dread. For many people, the dread is in working for compa-nies where they are constantly faced with a glass ceiling. In these scenarios, they already know how far they can go or how much money they can make. And the excitement is gone. It's like watching a movie in which you already know the ending. You can't get excited because you already know the outcome. That's why it's so important to discover one's purpose or life work because it removes the boredom in life and moves one toward being a happier person.

The way out of the drudgery is to acknowledge that you

are pregnant. Whether or not we can biologically conceive a baby, all of us are pregnant with ideas and dreams, and nobody else can bring these dreams and ideas into the world but us. They were given to us and they are ours. You may be aborting dreams and ideas just short of their being birthed into reality because you don't want the responsibility of caring for them and nurturing them; you don't want to see your dreams and aspirations die an early death.

However, it was the late Dr. Benjamin E. Mays, former president of Morehouse College and a great educator, who said, "The tragedy of life doesn't lie in not reaching your goal. The tragedy lies in having no goal to reach for. It isn't a calamity to die with dreams unfulfilled, but it is a calamity not to dream. Not failure, but low aim is sin." The essence of Mays' statement goes against the grain of what we've been taught—"go for it," "get it," "you must make it to the top." Who's top? It's not about the top. Top might not be for you. The real issue is, have you tapped into your potential?

In each of us is a sleeping giant of potentiality waiting to be tapped into, awakened, and energized. As we seek to become our best self and start living our dreams, there will always be somebody or something trying to hold us back. Someone will tell us that we can't do it. But no one knows better than us what we can do. Instead of going through life fulfilling other people's dreams, it's time to start living *our* dreams. This means answering the following: How much time do I spend on myself? How much time do I invest in myself? How many risks do I take to improve my position in life?

Now, why do you think people don't pursue their life's work or live up to their full potential? Most of us live our lives

153

according to somebody else's idea of what we should be doing. But achieving excellence is going as far as the mind will take you.

In Stephen Covey's national bestseller, *The Seven Habits of Highly Effective People,* he tells us that the first habit is to "begin with the end in mind." Most people don't pursue their life work because they can't see it. And when you can't see it you don't know what to do or where to start. I think this is why people who work in corporate settings crumble or fold when they hear about promotions, demotions, lateral moves, downsizing, mergers, acquisitions, technology upgrades, and bankruptcies. These types of changes signal to some workers, "You're in trouble" or "You may not have a job tomorrow." That's because they can't see themselves beyond that company. They just don't believe that there is a better life in the company or that there is really any life after that company.

This is also one of the main reasons why people stay in relationships that are unhealthy and that they are not happy with. They can't see themselves beyond the relationship or can't see themselves enjoying life without the other person. They can't see bigger and better things on the other side.

There are people who can't handle change or adversity in their lives, and they try to put it off. As a result, they get stuck at a certain point in life. These people think that whatever they are involved in, this is it for them, and this is all that they deserve. This is usually because this is all they have ever seen in life. They don't know anything else. Instead of stepping out on faith they just stay stuck in the same position, being complacent and satisfied with just having any job or relationship.

But if we are going to live out our dreams, then we have

to be able to see ourselves doing it. Imagining ourselves doing things we've never done may be difficult and challenging. It's not the problems, though, that we should concentrate on, it's the possibilities. In order to achieve excellence we must focus on our goals no matter what the changing tide. This is what faith concerns itself with: "The substance of things hoped for, the evidence of things not seen." (Heb. 11:1) Our dream may not be visible or tangible now. We may not be able to show it off now. But if we've already seen it in our mind, then it can come to pass. Goal setting is, therefore, critical. Where do we want to be one, two, five years from now?

One of the major reasons people have difficulty achieving excellence or living up to their potential, and why people can't see themselves beyond a particular position or situation, is fear.

Because of its gripping nature, fear is the most subtle and destructive of all human diseases. Yes, it is a disease, and it disguises itself as cancer, AIDS, heart disease, pneumonia, migraines, diarrhea, etc. Fear kills hopes; it ages and hospitalizes, paralyzes and cripples people. Some people won't take risks and step out on faith because of fear. Maybe they don't want to make a mistake; maybe they don't want to fall flat on their faces; maybe they are more concerned with looking good in other people's eyes. Maybe they just want to play it safe. Fear really profits no one. It keeps one from going forward. It holds one back. For many people, when change or adversity comes into their lives, it is fear that throws them off balance. They are afraid of the future and can't imagine positive things happening in their lives.

There is no benefit in allowing fear to hold us back. Fear

is making something real that doesn't exist by creating it in our minds. Many people are constipated with ideas and possibilities, because fear has seized them and told them that they cannot do something—it's too hard for them, it's not for them to have, or they're not good enough. And they believe it because what they are feeling and thinking seems to be real.

I once heard a story about a boy who, every day as he walked home from school, was chased and barked at by a dog. One day the boy decided that the next time the dog came after him he was going to hit him upside the head with a brick. Well, as he walked home that next time, sure enough, the dog started after him. As the boy was running away, he saw a brick and picked it up. He turned around with the brick in his hand, cocked behind his head, and as the dog got close to him, he realized that the dog didn't have any teeth.

Many of us go through life running from things that don't have any teeth—that can't hurt us, hold us back, or keep us from achieving excellence. All of us can probably attest to experiences when we were afraid to do something and when we finally did it, we realized that there had really been nothing to fear in the first place. As Franklin Delano Roosevelt said, "The only thing we have to fear is fear itself." Most fears are created in our minds. The mind is powerful, and it can slay a dragon on one hand and slay you on the other. The mind will play those kinds of tricks. That's why we have to be careful about which part of the mind we are going to live out of.

This is especially important for those in the African American community. Often when we don't land that job or get that promotion we blame it on racism. If it doesn't happen for us, we blame racism. Yes, racism is real, but so is fear. Maybe you weren't aggressive enough. Maybe you told yourself that you don't have what it takes. Maybe you thought, because I'm an African American I won't get it. Maybe you let your fear of what you thought to be real hold you back. But be careful because you do not want to end up having to say one day, "If I would've, could've, should've." Tell the fear to get out of the way.

How do you get rid of fear? Fear and low self-esteem are opposite sides of the same coin. Fear and low self-esteem are inseparable, Siamese twins. Have you ever noticed that when change comes, when things break away from what people are accustomed to, those who have low self-esteem always panic. Why? Because they don't believe in themselves. They don't believe they can make it through the new situation. Self-esteem is confidence and satisfaction with one's self and one's capabilities, no matter what.

I realize that in today's society—with all the pressures and competitiveness, soap operas, talk shows, and false, idealized media images—it's hard to feel good about one's self. We allow other people to define who we are. But no one ought to be allowed to define, categorize, or pigeonhole anyone because if we accept someone's definition of us, then we have given that person some control over our thinking and, ultimately, our behavior. We start living out of their definition of us. I have discovered that people with low self-esteem usually view their futures as hopeless. But without hope it is impossible to be motivated and achieve excellence.

In order to keep hope alive one must believe in one's self. This may require an attitude adjustment. I recommend two important qualities that a person nurture in their attitude in order to achieve excellence despite change and adversity—positivity and perseverance.

We live in a very negative society, and if we allow it, negativity can feed our fears; therefore, it's important to keep a positive frame of mind. This means that you may have to talk to yourself sometimes to build yourself up. Sometimes, if not most times, you will be the only person who is going to say anything good about you. Go ahead and take advantage of it. Boost yourself. Encourage yourself. When faced with adversity, tell yourself, "I can do this." "I can accomplish this." "I can do anything I want to."

The fact is nobody can improve you but you. It takes a lot of hard work to be positive when you are bombarded with constant negativity. The first place and best place to start is to watch less television.

It's hard to feel good or pumped up if you look at the news today, or even most entertainment shows, especially if you are an African American. The subliminal effect of TV on the mind is powerful. I seldom watch the news because I want to protect my psyche. I refuse to get to the point where I'm afraid of every young black male who looks a certain way. It is especially important not to watch the news just before retiring for bed, because you go to sleep with all negativity in your consciousness. You end up having bad dreams or restless sleep and wake up disoriented and irritable, which in turn affects your ability to perform. Don't let your mind be programmed with negative stuff, because it can make you a negative person. You are what you eat, and if you feed your psyche a lot of negativity you will be a negative person and a negative performer, and you will hamper your ability to achieve excellence. Therefore, turning off television programs that feed and contribute to your fear is essential.

Furthermore, in order to achieve excellence, then I recommend turning a deaf ear to people who talk only negatively, who are being influenced by the negative programming of the world. If you want to achieve excellence in spite of adversity, place yourself in environments or around people who help you grow, who contribute to your life's purpose and make you feel good about you. Listen to only those things that will begin to recondition your mind positively so that you can take on the world. Create a network of people in your life that you can count on to support you and be there for you when things don't look so well. I'm not saying you need people who will lie to you—none of us is so wonderful that we don't have any shortcomings. You need people who will be real with you, who will tell you the truth. All of us have gifts, talents, and abilities that enable us to make a difference in this world.

159

Therefore, it's essential to have around you people who will offer constructive criticism that challenges you to grow. This will require getting rid of all the flaky people in your life. You may have to do some life cleaning. I did, a few years ago. I realized that I had become so negative that I didn't need any more negative people around me. If I were going to become a more positive person, I would have to surround myself with more positive people who would be available to support and encourage me when I needed them. If you want to find out who these people are in your life, test them. If they don't show up when you call on them, or if they seldom have an encouraging word to say, then you may have to become unavailable for them.

I'm sure you've heard the saying, "One bad apple will spoil the whole bunch." Well, I can assure you that one bad person can spoil your whole life. Association does bring about assimilation. Nobody needs anyone who is going to hold them back or tear them down. Getting rid of negative people so their negativity doesn't rub off on you is certainly in your best interest.

Once the negatives have been diminished, then you have to keep pressing on. This is called perseverance. No matter how challenging or difficult some things may be, you have to keep going after your goal. Whatever your dream, idea, vision, aspiration, you have to keep working on it. You may not get it right at first; you will make mistakes in the process. We all do. You will probably get knocked down or get knocked back occasionally. But you must be resilient and keep moving. If you get dismissed from a job or get demoted or are discriminated against, don't let it deter you from your goals. In life it matters how you look at the cup—whether it's half empty or half full, whether it's a step back or a blessing in disguise. Nothing should keep any of us from reaching for our goals. My father used to say, "If you can't run, walk. If you can't walk, crawl. If you can't crawl, then just do something, but by all means keep moving." Who's in a rush, after all? Just keep moving. The race is not to the swift, nor to the strong, but to those who endure till the end.

Even in the face of adversity, to achieve excellence means to hold on and to hold out. Rest if you must, but don't quit. Even if you give out, that's okay. Just don't give up. Keep pressing your way. Keep your eyes on the prize and hold on. Excellence is not about who outdid whom or who surpassed whom, it's about going through and coming out still focused on fulfilling your life's purpose.

A story is told about a ship that was caught in a fog so deep that you could not see your hand in front of your face. This ship was known to be the fastest ship on the ocean. On this particular day, however, the fog was so thick that the passengers were afraid. The boat was going too fast in the fog. They kept thinking that they would run aground or hit another ship, but the boat kept going full steam ahead.

The passengers called a meeting and demanded that the ship slow down because it was endangering their lives. The midshipman tried desperately to allay their fears, but all they could see was the fog. The passengers tried for a second time to convince the midshipman to slow down the boat, but to no avail.

Finally, the midshipman calmed the passengers, and while they were quiet they heard a voice saying "full steam ahead, full steam ahead." The passengers demanded to see the captain and the midshipman pointed upward toward the crow's nest, forty feet above the fog, and there was the captain saying "full steam ahead, full steam ahead."

So many lives are caught in the fog—the fog of uncertainty, fear, indifference, negativity, of sexism and racism, and of isolation. But in the crow's nest there is a voice crying "full steam ahead."

So let no fire consume your hopes for a brighter tomorrow, let no water wash away your dreams and aspirations. Let no fear dominate you and hold you back. If you want to achieve excellence, it's up to you.

REMEMBERING
OUR AFRICAN AMERICAN
HERITAGE

I stand before you today as one who is tremendously proud. I am proud that I share in the rich history and heritage of a people who, in spite of the odds, have risen to the task and are still moving forward. I am proud that even though people have sought to rewrite history, and even to redefine a people, the truth has prevailed, and more and more those in authority are having to face the truth. I also realize that the truth can sometimes be very painful for people who have made it their life mission to seek to bend and even destroy the truth. But it is true that "Truth stands the test of time; lies are soon exposed." (Prov. 12:19)

We are now experiencing the dawning of a new day in America. It is a day of new possibilities and new challenges for African Americans. Even though many of the battles of the past are still with us, no one can deny that we have come a long way. In 1965, the year of the Voting Rights Act, we had less than six hundred black elected officials in the entire country. Today, there are more than six thousand African American elected officials. Let me hasten to add, however, that this is still less than 2 percent of the total number of elected officials in this nation.

I am encouraged and excited because great and notable gains have been made in the political arena. We have African Americans serving as speakers in state legislatures and as state court judges. We have African Americans whose names have appeared on U.S. currency. An African American has served as governor of one of the old confederate states.

On the other hand, I am sad because the U.S. Senate has only one African American among its ranks, and it is here that major decisions governing the lives of some forty million African Americans are being made. Something is seriously wrong when this injustice can continue, and the political process does not offer any resolution. When this is coupled with the fact that many African Americans have either forgotten where they come from, or simply don't want to remember, it makes the problem even more serious.

I do not have to tell you that the Civil Rights Commission has become the Civil Wrongs Commission, and Affirmative Action has become Affirmative Distractions, and that the battle is not over. Surely, there are many African Americans who have concluded that we have arrived. My question is, arrived where? Where are we as a people? Where is our culture, our history, our legacy?

It has been said, "He who does not know history is doomed to repeat it." We as African Americans must put forth a concerted effort to know and to write our own history. No longer can the FBI and ill-intentioned journalists and out-of-touch scholars be allowed to write our history. We have the knowledge, the know-how, the resources, and we were there. But when we allow others to define who we are and describe our experience, we invite distortion and half-truth.

It is not an accident that African American history has been left out of major textbooks in America. We must do something about this, and we must not wait for someone else to do for us what we ought to be doing ourselves. For too long, our people have been left in the dark about who we are and our rich and noble history. We must tell our story to give us the boost that we so desperately need.

Our history tells us that Christopher Columbus did not discover America. Hundreds of years before Columbus, African shipbuilders and sailors had journeyed to America many times. This has been verified by the remains of African skulls and artifacts found in several states and in Mexico. Our history also conveys that Africa is the birthplace of all of humanity and that the first university in the world was in Africa—it was called the Grand Lodge of Wa'at. The saying "Man, know thyself" did not come from Plato, or Socrates, but was inscribed on the wall at the Grand Lodge of Wa'at hundreds of years before Plato. This leads to the conclusion that the Greeks studied under the Egyptians, and we must constantly remind the world that Egypt is in Africa. Our history also reminds us that the Shrine of the Black Madonna is still viewed in Russia, Spain, and Poland and is frequented by Pope John Paul II. Furthermore, our history tells us that when King Herod ordered the young male children to be killed,

Joseph and Mary took Jesus to Egypt, not to Europe, because they wanted to blend in with other dark-skinned people.

I've shared these facts to point out that history has been distorted and twisted to satisfy a few people in power who have wanted to remain in power. But it is our responsibility to stay informed so that we can keep our people informed. Information means power, and power is what the power structure wants us to believe we don't have, and yet nothing could be further from the truth. We have never been a powerless people. We have taken what others have discarded and turned them into things of value. We took scraps and made quilts and tables and art. We took discarded lives, mixed them with a little tender loving care, and created the Jesse Jacksons, Harriet Tubmans, Barbara Jordans, and the Nelson Mandelas.

We must continue to empower our people with knowledge. Education is still the key to our success, but we cannot teach that which we do not know ourselves. Therefore, we must first get all the knowledge we can. We must know that ours is a great tradition. We are the sons and daughters of great kings and queens, heroes and heroines. We come from a strong tradition of respect for family and the community where we live. We are created to be molders, builders, and founders of great civilizations. African Americans had talent that established the first mathematical system known to man; talent that was reading the heavens before there was ever a telescope; talent that founded the American Red Cross; talent that built institutions of higher learning from selling sweet potato pies and peanuts; talent that even invented ice cream and the golf tee. We are more than cotton pickers and ditch diggers and carriers of water. We are scholars, philosophers, teachers, inventors, doctors, lawyers, managers, manufacturers, and scientists.

We must teach our children that we cannot afford to waste this history on fast living, pump-up tennis shoes, Starter jackets, and arrow hairdos. We must insist that our children be educated about the truth, and we must be a part of the education process. We must go beyond traditional textbooks and make sure that good books about our history and heritage are readily available. This means that all of us must be conscientious about reading and getting away from the television where the images of who we are are often confusing, to say the least.

How do you think that the system was able to get us to start killing each other? They found every isolated case of a black-on-black crime and made sure that 100,000 people saw it on television, 50,000 read about it in the paper, and 150,000 heard about it on the radio. Our young people started believing this was who we are, and soon, the cases were not isolated but the norm, and black-on-black crime became a way of life.

We must dismiss the notion that the majority press is going to portray us in a positive manner. We must face the fact that it is not in their interest to do so. They know that if the truth got out it would reveal that the majority of our women are not on welfare, the majority of our men are not behind bars, the majority of our young men do not commit murder, the majority of our people do want a job, and the majority of our people do want to be self-sufficient and independent.

They tell us that, nationally, unemployment among black

men is around 12.7 percent, and that is bad. That is twice as high as the unemployment rate of whites. But this also means that 88 percent of black men are working and want to work. True enough, almost 30 percent of black families nationally live below the poverty line, and that is terrible, but it also means that 70 percent live above the poverty line. It's all a matter of the glass being half full or half empty, and the system wants us to feel half empty. But too many people have fought, bled, and died so that I would feel good about myself rather than take on a defeatist attitude. We've come too far to let a few statistics beat us down and dictate the course of our future.

It is the intent of those in the power structure to portray average African Americans as weak, lazy, violent, uneducated, complacent, apathetic, and in some cases even uncivilized. And unless those of us who have made it are able, through our own means, to show and tell the positive side of our people, we will become part of the problem rather than part of the solution.

Admittedly, though, there are those who sit on the sideline (the apathetic people), those who don't know what's going on (the uninformed and in-the-dark people), and those who get involved (the enlightened and dedicated people). It is clear that the apathetic sideliners will not advance the struggle because they think that this is the way it is and always will be. The don't-know-what-happened, uninformed people can't take us anywhere because they don't know where to start, so they believe any road will get them there. But the enlightened and dedicated people will move us forward because they see what needs to be done and they do it.

If our history teaches us anything, it is that change takes place when people realize that if the struggle is to be advanced, then they are going to have to do it. We've got to start with ourselves. We can no longer wait for "somebody else" to do for us what we should do for ourselves because "somebody else" is dead. If you don't do it, then "somebody's" first cousin, Mr. Nobody, will.

In order to reclaim our African American heritage, we need those people who are not afraid to speak the truth and show the hypocrisies. We need people who value truth and honesty and who are willing to take a risk sometimes and bite the bullet rather than kowtow to corporate leaders. We need men and women who will challenge the double standards of one rule for whites and another rule for blacks. Certainly this is not an easy task, but as Frederick Douglass, noted black liberator, reminds us, "Where there is no struggle, there can be no progress." Certainly struggle has always been a part of our history. Somebody had to pay the price for us to be where we are. Somebody bled and somebody died. Somebody spent time in jail and we must never forget this. We must teach generations after us to value who we are and what we have achieved and how we overcame, or they will be born, raised, live, and die in ignorance of who they are. We must lay down our personality differences and lock our arms together, and use our minds creatively to build a more knowledgeable African American community. In order not to repeat mistakes of the past, we must realize where we are, and then act to make life better for all God's children.

We can no longer afford to be like Christopher Columbus. He didn't know where he was going when he got started.

When he got there, he didn't know where he was. And when he got back, he couldn't tell anyone where he had been. We've got to know where we are, who we are, whose we are, and where we are going.

Someone once said that he who controls our children ultimately controls us. Our children, then, are the most important investments we can make in securing our African American heritage as well as the future. It's time that we stop giving our children things and start giving them ourselves, because every day our children are crying out for our love and attention. Drugs and gangs and fashions are mere substitutes for the lack of love and attention we give to our children. If you ask children why they join gangs, most will tell you that they find more love, attention, and acceptance in gangs than they've ever received at home. But this has not always been the story in the African American community. When the traditional nuclear family failed to sustain our children, there was always the extended family to back it up. But now that society has redefined family to include the corporation to the exclusion of the nuclear and extended family, too many of our African American brothers and sisters have become so caught up in pleasing the boss and making a living that we seldom leave time to teach our children how to live. Then we have the nerve to say that something is wrong with our children. No, nothing's wrong with them. They are just looking for what any child needs—love. Something is wrong with us because we're not giving it to them.

If ever there was a time to reclaim who we truly are as African Americans, now is that time. It's time to restore our sense of family and community. It's time to recapture the minds and imaginations of our young people, which means it's time to tell the true story of our history and our heritage. We must build from our proud and noble heritage.

African Americans are a great people, and we must keep holding our heads high because in our veins flows the courage of Harriet Tubman, the perseverance of Mary McLeod Bethune, the inspiration of Booker T. Washington, the vision of W. E. B. DuBois, the military genius of Hannibal, and the unconquerable beauty of Cleopatra and Queen Nefertiti. In our veins is the creativity of Paul Robeson, the bravery of Malcolm X, the hope of Whitney Young, and the challenge of the unforgettable Roy Wilkins. Tell our children that in their veins is the compassion of Martin L. King Jr., the intellectual astuteness of Dr. George Washington Carver, the business genius of Madame C. J. Walker, the political savvy of Jesse Jackson, and, yes, the convictions of Nelson Mandela. We have a heritage to reclaim and a history to preserve.

With hope above to inspire us, faith around us to encourage us, convictions beneath us to sustain us, love within us to guide us, and with God in front of us to direct us, we will overcome.

A CALL

FOR

GOOD SAMARITANS

It has been said that there are three types of people in the
world: those who sit on the sideline and watch what happens, the few who get involved and make things happen,
and the overwhelming majority who don't know what happened. I am delighted to know and affirm that there are some
in our nation who have been on the cutting edge of making
things happen. As we move closer to the twenty-first century,
this same momentum will be critical to the transformation of
this nation from its present state of self-centered individualism to one that truly embraces the interrelatedness of all of
life.

If we take an honest look at the present plight of our nation, we see that our inner cities are becoming breeding
grounds for violent and criminal lifestyles. Our families are
being tormented by division and disunity. Our marriages are
being replaced by divorce proceedings and alternative
lifestyles. Our public schools are being transformed into

battlegrounds by defiant and rebellious children. Our streets have become homes for the dejected and rejected. Our hospitals have become the exclusive domain of those who can afford them. Our funeral homes are being flooded with victims of drug deals gone bad, and all of this has unfolded before our very eyes. It's as if we have stopped up our ears, shut our eyes, and turned our heads away. I surmise that the reason our nation has overlooked our poor, deprived our children, neglected our elderly, locked up our young, exploited our women, and ignored God is because many in the church community have barely lifted a hand to really get involved with the problems and concerns that are in dire need of attention.

I am compelled to ask, where was the church when those on Capitol Hill said that we do not have money to take the homeless off the streets, even though when the savings and loans banks got in trouble, they found over $150 billion to bail them out? Where was the church when they said that we do not have money to help the working poor, even though when Chrysler got in trouble they managed to find over $50 million? Is it not important to us that there are a host of victims that lie helplessly on the road of life waiting for someone to stop and comfort them? The 23 million functionally illiterate, the more than 3 million homeless, especially the one out of three high school dropouts, and a host of other victims of our society challenge the church once again, as during the Reformation and the civil rights movement, to come out of the pews, roll up its sleeves, and reach out beyond the beautiful stained glass windows. They challenge the church to identify with the poor, stand up for righteousness, and be counted on the Lord's side.

It is time for us to stop playing church. We have had ample rehearsal time. Now is the time for the church of God to get on center stage and take the leading role. I do not believe that God intended for the church to be the taillight, bringing up the rear. God has always intended for the church to be the headlight, pointing and showing the way.

It is a critical time in the history of our nation because our future seems imperiled. There are those who have already written the eulogy for an entire generation of young people, and some young people from that generation have even written their own funeral services. We can ill afford for the religious community to be paralyzed at such a crucial time. The time is past for timid, docile, cowardly, reticent Christians. We need more risk-takers.

This is why Jesus' parable about the Good Samaritan in Luke 10:30–35 is so powerful and pertinent. In that story, Jesus tells of a man who had been traveling from Jerusalem to Jericho by way of the Jericho Road and had fallen among thieves. The thieves beat and stripped the man of his clothes and left him for dead on the side of the road. The first two men who approached where the robbed and beaten man lay, a priest and a Levite, passed by on the other side without rendering any assistance. It was a third man, a Samaritan, who stopped and rendered aid to the helpless man. We are not told why the priest and Levite did not stop to help, but perhaps they were afraid of what could happen to them. Most of us, if we are honest, are just like the priest and Levite in the parable; we opt to pass by difficult situations and problems that confront us because we are intimidated by the thought of taking a risk.

Instead of addressing the reasons people so often pass by, I want to focus on the act of the Good Samaritan and glean some insight into why it's so important that we do not pass by; we must reach out with a helping hand to make our communities much better places in which to live.

First, I belief that the Good Samaritan stopped to assist this helpless man on the Jericho Road because he realized that time was of the essence. He could have been on his way to a very important meeting where people were waiting for him, or he could have just had some urgent errands to run, but he took the time to stop. Perhaps he realized that this was a problem that needed attention now, not later.

Furthermore, this Samaritan knew he didn't have time to sit around and decide what to do. He knew he had to help the man then or it would be too late. So often we waste a lot of time calling together commissions to study a problem and then we create another commission to study the commission that studied the problem. But the problems only get worse. We know the problems and most of the time we know what the real solutions are. It's time for us to get busy and go about God's business. God has need of workers to till His soil today.

Second, the Samaritan focused more on the power he had rather than on his own sense of helplessness. Oftentimes people become paralyzed by the notion that "I am only one person who can't really make a difference," but so was this Samaritan. He could have very easily excused himself by saying that the man on the side of the road is the victim of a greater and more complex societal problem. However, I can imagine that the Samaritan must have said to himself, "Although I am only one person, I am one person who cannot do everything, but I can do something. What I can do, I ought to do, and what I ought to do, by God's grace I will do it." Rosa Parks was just one lady, but because she sat down, a whole race of people could stand up to confront racism and inequality.

The good news is that when one individual does something good, it can create a domino effect. Sometimes people just need to know or see that someone else is doing something. Everybody has the power to do something to help those who have become victims of our society. The songwriter was right who said, "If I can help somebody as I pass along, if I can cheer somebody with a word or song, if I can show somebody he's traveling wrong, then my living shall not be in vain."

And finally, the Samaritan gave of himself. He didn't call on anybody else. He didn't even pick up his cellular phone to call 911. Too many of us would prefer to call someone else or pay someone else to do a job that we can do ourselves.

If we look around we can affirm the fact that we have a lot of programs that are designed to help the less fortunate. But one of the biggest problems is not always the lack of available money to get these programs off the ground but the lack of people power. I don't know of any program or organization that ever made real progress without people who were willing to give personal time and attention. The bottom line is this: people just need other people.

It is so good to know that we serve a God who is not selfish but was willing to come out of the confines of His holy place to show us the way—for God so loved the world that He gave Himself through the person of Jesus Christ.